Yasmina Reza

PLAYS ONE

Yasmina Reza is French, based in Paris. Her works have all been multi-award-winning critical and popular international successes. Her plays (*Conversations after a Burial*, *The Passage of Winter*, *'Art'*, *The Unexpected Man*, *Life x 3* and *A Spanish Play*) have been produced worldwide and translated into thirty-five languages. She has translated *La Metamorphose* (Stephen Berkoff's version of Kafka's *Metamorphosis*), which was directed by Roman Polanski. Novels include *Hammerklavier*, *Desolation*, *Adam Haberberg*. Film: *Le Pique-nique de Lulu Kreutz*, directed by Didier Martiny.

Christopher Hampton was born in the Azores in 1946. He wrote his first play, *When Did You Last See My Mother?*, at the age of eighteen. His work for the theatre and cinema includes *The Philanthropist*, *Savages*, *Tales from Hollywood*, translations from Ibsen, Molière and Chekhov, and the screenplays *Dangerous Liaisons*, *The Quiet American*, *Carrington*, *The Secret Agent* and *Imagining Argentina*, the last three of which he also directed.

by the same author

HAMMERKLAVIER
THE GOD OF CARNAGE

YASMINA REZA

Plays One

'Art'
The Unexpected Man
Conversations after a Burial
Life x 3

faber and faber

This collection first published in 2005
by Faber and Faber Limited
Bloomsbury House
74–77 Great Russell Street
London WC1B 3DA
Published in the United States by Faber and Faber Inc.
an affiliate of Farrar, Straus and Giroux LLC, New York

Typeset by Country Setting, Kingsdown, Kent CT14 8ES
Printed in the UK by CPI Bookmarque, Croydon

4 6 8 10 9 7 5

Contents

'ART'

'**Art**' in this translation was first performed at Wyndham's Theatre, London, on 15 October 1996. The cast was as follows:

Marc Albert Finney
Serge Tom Courtenay
Yvan Ken Stott

Directed by Matthew Warchus
Designed by Mark Thompson
Lighting by Hugh Vanstone
Music by   Gary Yershon
Produced by David Pugh and Sean Connery

Characters

Marc

Serge

Yvan

The main room of a flat.

A single set. As stripped-down and neutral as possible.

The scenes unfold, successively, at Serge's,
Yvan's and Marc's.

Nothing changes, except for the painting on the wall.

Marc, alone.

Marc My friend Serge has bought a painting. It's a canvas about five foot by four: white. The background is white and, if you screw up your eyes, you can make out some fine white diagonal lines.

Serge is one of my oldest friends.

He's done very well for himself, he's a dermatologist and he's keen on *art*.

On Monday I went to see the painting; Serge had actually got hold of it on the Saturday, but he'd been lusting after it for several months.

This white painting with white lines.

At Serge's.

At floor level, a white canvas with fine white diagonal scars. Serge looks at his painting, thrilled. Marc looks at the painting. Serge looks at Marc looking at the painting.

Long silence: from both of them, a whole range of wordless emotions.

Marc Expensive?

Serge Two hundred thousand.

Marc Two hundred thousand?

Serge Huntingdon would take it off my hands for two hundred and twenty.

Marc Who's that?

7

Serge Huntingdon?

Marc Never heard of him.

Serge Huntingdon! The Huntingdon Gallery!

Marc The Huntingdon Gallery would take it off your hands for two hundred and twenty?

Serge No, not the Gallery. Him. Huntingdon himself. For his own collection.

Marc Then why didn't Huntingdon buy it?

Serge It's important for them to sell to private clients. That's how the market circulates.

Marc Mm hm . . .

Serge Well?

Marc . . .

Serge You're not in the right place. Look at it from this angle.
   Can you see the lines?

Marc What's the name of the . . .?

Serge Painter. Antrios.

Marc Well known?

Serge Very. Very!

   Pause.

Marc Serge, you haven't bought this painting for two hundred thousand francs?

Serge You don't understand, that's what it costs. It's an Antrios.

Marc You haven't bought this painting for two hundred thousand francs?

Serge I might have known you'd miss the point.

Marc You paid two hundred thousand francs for this shit?

Serge, as if alone.

Serge My friend Marc's an intelligent enough fellow, I've always valued our relationship, he has a good job, he's an aeronautical engineer, but he's one of those new-style intellectuals who are not only enemies of modernism but seem to take some sort of incomprehensible pride in running it down . . .

  In recent years these nostalgia-merchants have become quite breathtakingly arrogant.

Same pair. Same place. Same painting.
  Pause.

Serge What do you mean, 'this shit'?

Marc Serge, where's your sense of humour? Why aren't you laughing? . . . It's fantastic, you buying this painting.

  Marc laughs. Serge remains stony.

Serge I don't care how fantastic you think it is, I don't mind if you laugh, but I would like to know what you mean by 'this shit'.

Marc You're taking the piss!

Serge No, I'm not. By whose standards is it shit? If you call something shit, you need to have some criterion to judge it by.

Marc Who are you talking to? Who do you think you're talking to? Hello! . . .

9

Serge You have no interest whatsoever in contemporary painting, you never have had. This is a field about which you know absolutely nothing, so how can you assert that any given object, which conforms to laws you don't understand, is shit?

Marc Because it is. It's shit. I'm sorry.

Serge, alone.

Serge He doesn't like the painting.
Fine . . .
But there was no warmth in the way he reacted.
No attempt.
No warmth when he dismissed it out of hand.
Just that vile, pretentious laugh.
A real know-all laugh.
I hated that laugh.

Marc, alone.

Marc It's a complete mystery to me, Serge buying this painting. It's unsettled me, it's filled me with some indefinable unease.
    When I left his place, I had to take three capsules of Gelsemium 9X which Paula recommended – Gelsemium or Ignatia, she said, Gelsemium or Ignatia, which do you prefer? I mean, how the hell should I know? – because I couldn't begin to understand how Serge, my friend, could have bought that picture.
    Two hundred thousand francs!
    He's comfortably off, but he's hardly rolling in money.
    Comfortable, no more, just comfortable. And he spends two hundred grand on a white painting.

I must go and see Yvan, he's a friend of ours, I have to discuss this with Yvan. Mind you, Yvan's a very tolerant bloke, which, of course, when it comes to relationships, is the worst thing you can be.

Yvan's very tolerant because he couldn't care less.

If Yvan tolerates the fact that Serge has spent two hundred grand on some piece of white shit, it's because he couldn't care less about Serge.

Obviously.

At Yvan's.
On the wall, some daub.
Yvan is on all fours with his back to us. He seems to be looking for something underneath a piece of furniture. As he does so, he turns to introduce himself.

Yvan I'm Yvan.

I'm a bit tense at the moment, because, having spent my life in textiles, I've just found a new job as a sales agent for a wholesale stationery business.

People like me. My professional life has always been a failure and I'm getting married in a couple of weeks. She's a lovely intelligent girl from a good family.

Marc enters. Yvan has resumed his search and has his back to him.

Marc What are you doing?

Yvan I'm looking for the top of my pen.

Time passes.

Marc All right, that's enough.

Yvan I had it five minutes ago.

Marc It doesn't matter.

Yvan Yes, it does.

Marc gets down on his knees to help him look. Both of them spend some time looking. Marc straightens up.

Marc Stop it. Buy another one.

Yvan It's a felt-tip, they're special, they'll write on any surface . . . It's just infuriating. Objects, I can't tell you how much they infuriate me. I had it in my hand five minutes ago.

Marc Are you going to live here?

Yvan Do you think it's suitable for a young couple?

Marc Young couple! Ha, ha . . .

Yvan Try not to laugh like that in front of Catherine.

Marc How's the stationery business?

Yvan All right. I'm learning.

Marc You've lost weight.

Yvan A bit. I'm pissed off about that top. It'll all dry up. Sit down.

Marc If you go on looking for that top, I'm leaving.

Yvan OK, I'll stop. You want something to drink?

Marc A Perrier, if you have one.
Have you seen Serge lately?

Yvan No. Have you?

Marc Yesterday.

Yvan Is he well?

Marc Very.
He's just bought a painting.

Yvan Oh yes?

Marc Mm.

Yvan Nice?

Marc White.

Yvan White?

Marc White.

Imagine a canvas about five foot by four . . . with a white background . . . completely white in fact . . . with fine white diagonal stripes . . . you know . . . and maybe another horizontal white line, towards the bottom . . .

Yvan How can you see them?

Marc What?

Yvan These white lines. If the background's white, how can you see the lines?

Marc You just do. Because I suppose the lines are slightly grey, or vice versa, or anyway there are degrees of white! There's more than one kind of white!

Yvan Don't get upset. Why are you getting upset?

Marc You immediately start quibbling. Why can't you let me finish?

Yvan All right. Go on.

Marc Right. So, you have an idea of what the painting looks like.

Yvan I think so, yes.

Marc Now you have to guess how much Serge paid for it.

Yvan Who's the painter?

Marc Antrios. Have you heard of him?

13

Yvan No. Is he fashionable?

Marc I knew you were going to ask me that!

Yvan Well, it's logical . . .

Marc No, it isn't logical . . .

Yvan Of course it's logical, you ask me to guess the price, you know very well the price depends on how fashionable the painter might be . . .

Marc I'm not asking you to apply a whole set of critical standards, I'm not asking you for a professional valuation, I'm asking you what you, Yvan, would give for a white painting tarted up with a few off-white stripes.

Yvan Bugger all.

Marc Right. And what about Serge? Pick a figure at random.

Yvan Ten thousand francs.

Marc Ha!

Yvan Fifty thousand.

Marc Ha!

Yvan A hundred thousand.

Marc Keep going.

Yvan A hundred and fifty? Two hundred?!

Marc Two hundred. Two hundred grand.

Yvan No!

Marc Yes.

Yvan Two hundred grand?

Marc Two hundred grand.

Yvan Has he gone crazy?

Marc Looks like it.

Slight pause.

Yvan All the same . . .

Marc What do you mean, all the same?

Yvan If it makes him happy . . . he can afford it . . .

Marc So that's what you think, is it?

Yvan Why? What do you think?

Marc You don't understand the seriousness of this, do you?

Yvan Er . . . no.

Marc It's strange how you're missing the basic point of this story. All you can see is externals. You don't understand the seriousness of it.

Yvan What is the seriousness of it?

Marc Don't you understand what this means?

Yvan Would you like a cashew nut?

Marc Don't you see that suddenly, in some grotesque way, Serge fancies himself as a 'collector'.

Yvan Well . . .

Marc From now on, our friend Serge is one of the great connoisseurs.

Yvan Bollocks.

Marc Well, of course it's bollocks. You can't buy your way in that cheap. But that's what *he* thinks.

Yvan Oh, I see.

Marc Doesn't that upset you?

Yvan No. Not if it makes him happy.

Marc 'If it makes him happy.' What's that supposed to mean?

What sort of a philosophy is that, 'If it makes him happy'?

Yvan As long as it's not doing any harm to anyone else . . .

Marc But it is. It's doing harm to me! I'm disturbed, I'm disturbed, more than that, I'm hurt, yes, I am, I'm fond of Serge, and to see him let himself be ripped off and lose every ounce of discernment through sheer snobbery . . .

Yvan I don't know why you're so surprised. He's always haunted galleries in the most absurd way, he's always been an exhibition freak.

Marc He's always been a freak, but a freak with a sense of humour. You see, basically, what really upsets me is that you can't have a laugh with him any more.

Yvan I'm sure you can.

Marc You can't!

Yvan Have you tried?

Marc Of course I've tried. I laughed. Heartily. What do you think I did? He didn't crack a smile.

Mind you, two hundred grand, I suppose it might be hard to see the funny side.

Yvan Yes.

They laugh.

I'll make him laugh.

Marc I'd be amazed. Any more nuts?

Yvan He'll laugh, you just wait.

At Serge's.
  Serge is with Yvan. The painting isn't there.

Serge . . . and you get on with the in-laws?

Yvan Wonderfully. As far as they're concerned, I'm some berk tottering from one dodgy job to another and now I'm groping my way into the world of vellum . . . This thing on my hand, what is it?

  Serge examines it.

Is it serious?

Serge No.

Yvan Oh, good. How are things?

Serge Nothing. Lot of work. Exhausted.
  It's nice to see you. You never phone.

Yvan I don't like to disturb you.

Serge You're joking. You just speak to my secretary and I'll call you back right away.

Yvan I suppose so.
  Your place gets more and more monastic . . .

  Serge laughs.

Serge Yes!
  Seen Marc recently?

Yvan Not recently, no.
  Have you?

Serge Two or three days ago.

Yvan Is he all right?

Serge Yes. More or less.

Yvan Oh?

Serge No, he's all right.

Yvan I talked to him on the phone last week, he seemed all right.

Serge Well, he is. He's all right.

Yvan You seemed to be implying he wasn't all right.

Serge On the contrary, I said he was all right.

Yvan More or less, you said.

Serge Yes, more or less. More or less all right.

Long silence. Yvan wanders around the room.

Yvan You been out? Seen anything?

Serge No. I can't afford to go out.

Yvan Oh?

Serge (*cheerfully*) I'm ruined.

Yvan Oh?

Serge You want to see something special? Would you like to?

Yvan Of course I would. Show me.

Serge exits and returns with the Antrios, which he turns round and sets down in front of Yvan.
 Yvan looks at the painting and, strangely enough, doesn't manage the hearty laugh he'd predicted.
 A long pause, while Yvan studies the painting and Serge studies Yvan.

Oh, yes. Yes, yes.

Serge Antrios.

Yvan Yes, yes.

Serge It's a seventies Antrios. Worth mentioning. He's going through a similar phase now, but this one's from the seventies.

Yvan Yes, yes.
Expensive?

Serge In absolute terms, yes. In fact, no.
You like it?

Yvan Oh, yes, yes, yes.

Serge Plain.

Yvan Plain, yes . . . Yes . . . And at the same time . . .

Serge Magnetic.

Yvan Mm . . . yes . . .

Serge You don't really get the resonance just at the moment.

Yvan Well, a bit . . .

Serge No, you don't. You have to come back in the middle of the day. That resonance you get from something monochromatic, it doesn't really happen under artificial light.

Yvan Mm hm.

Serge Not that it is actually monochromatic.

Yvan No! . . .
How much was it?

Serge Two hundred thousand.

Yvan Very reasonable.

Serge Very.

Silence. Suddenly Serge bursts out laughing, immediately followed by Yvan. Both of them roar with laughter.

Crazy, or what?

Yvan Crazy!

Serge Two hundred grand!

Hearty laughter. They stop. They look at each other. They start again. Then stop.
   They've calmed down.

Serge You know Marc's seen this painting.

Yvan Oh?

Serge Devastated.

Yvan Oh?

Serge He told me it was shit. A completely inappropriate description.

Yvan Absolutely.

Serge You can't call this shit.

Yvan No.

Serge You can say, 'I don't get it, I can't grasp it,' you can't say, 'It's shit.'

Yvan You've seen his place.

Serge Nothing to see.
   It's like yours, it's . . . what I mean is, you couldn't care less.

Yvan His taste is classical, he likes things classical, what do you expect . . .

Serge He started in with this sardonic laugh . . . Not a trace of charm . . . Not a trace of humour.

Yvan You know Marc is moody, there's nothing new about that . . .

Serge He has no sense of humour. With you, I can laugh. With him, I'm like a block of ice.

Yvan It's true he's a bit gloomy at the moment.

Serge I don't blame him for not responding to this painting, he hasn't the training, there's a whole apprenticeship you have to go through, which he hasn't, either because he's never wanted to or because he has no particular instinct for it, none of that matters, no, what I blame him for is his tone of voice, his complacency, his tactlessness.

I blame him for his insensitivity. I don't blame him for not being interested in modern Art, I couldn't give a toss about that, I like him for other reasons . . .

Yvan And he likes you!

Serge No, no, no, no, I felt it the other day, a kind of . . . a kind of condescension . . . contempt with a really bitter edge . . .

Yvan No, surely not!

Serge Oh, yes! Don't keep trying to smooth things over. Where d'you get this urge to be the great reconciler of the human race? Why don't you admit that Marc is atrophying? If he hasn't already atrophied.

Silence.

At Marc's.
On the wall, a figurative painting: a landscape seen through a window.

Yvan We had a laugh.

Marc You had a laugh?

Yvan We had a laugh. Both of us. We had a laugh.
I promise you on Catherine's life, we had a good laugh,
both of us, together.

Marc You told him it was shit and you had a good laugh.

Yvan No, I didn't tell him it was shit, we laughed
spontaneously.

Marc You arrived, you looked at the painting and you
laughed. And then he laughed.

Yvan Yes. If you like. We talked a bit, then it was more
or less as you described.

Marc A genuine laugh, was it?

Yvan Perfectly genuine.

Marc Well, then, I've made a mistake. Good. I'm really
pleased to hear it.

Yvan It was even better than you think. It was Serge
who laughed first.

Marc It was Serge who laughed first . . .

Yvan Yes.

Marc He laughed first and you joined in.

Yvan Yes.

Marc But what made him laugh?

Yvan He laughed because he sensed I was about to
laugh. If you like, he laughed to put me at my ease.

Marc It doesn't count if he laughed first.
If he laughed first, it was to defuse your laughter.
It means it wasn't a genuine laugh.

Yvan It was a genuine laugh.

Marc It may have been a genuine laugh, but it wasn't for the right reason.

Yvan What is the right reason? I'm confused.

Marc He wasn't laughing because his painting is ridiculous; you and he weren't laughing for the same reasons – you were laughing at the painting and he was laughing to ingratiate himself, to put himself on your wavelength, to show you that on top of being an aesthete who can spend more on a painting than you earn in a year, he's still your same old subversive mate who likes a good laugh.

Yvan Mm hm . . .

A brief silence.

You know . . .

Marc Yes . . .

Yvan This is going to amaze you . . .

Marc Go on . . .

Yvan I didn't like the painting . . . but I didn't actually hate it.

Marc Well, of course. You can't hate what's invisible, you can't hate nothing.

Yvan No, no, it has something . . .

Marc What do you mean?

Yvan It has something. It's not nothing.

Marc You're joking.

Yvan I'm not as harsh as you. It's a work of art, there's a system behind it.

23

Marc A system?

Yvan A system.

Marc What system?

Yvan It's the completion of a journey . . .

Marc Ha, ha, ha!

Yvan It wasn't painted by accident, it's a work of art which stakes its claim as part of a trajectory . . .

Marc Ha, ha, ha!

Yvan All right, laugh.

Marc You're parroting out all Serge's nonsense. From him, it's heartbreaking, from you it's just comical!

Yvan You know, Marc, this complacency, you want to watch out for it. You're getting bitter, it's not very attractive.

Marc Good. The older I get, the more offensive I hope to become.

Yvan Great.

Marc A system!

Yvan You're impossible to talk to.

Marc There's a system behind it! . . . You look at this piece of shit, but never mind, never mind, there's a system behind it! . . . You reckon there's a system behind this landscape? (*He indicates the painting on his wall.*) No, uh? Too evocative. Too expressive. Everything's on the canvas! No scope for a system! . . .

Yvan I'm glad you're enjoying yourself.

Marc Yvan, look, speak for yourself. Describe your feelings to me.

Yvan I felt a resonance.

Marc You felt a resonance? . . .

Yvan You're denying that I'm capable of appreciating this painting on my own account.

Marc Of course I am.

Yvan Well, why?

Marc Because I know you. Because, apart from your disastrous indulgence, you're quite sane.

Yvan I wish I could say the same for you.

Marc Yvan, look me in the eye.

Yvan I'm looking at you.

Marc Were you moved by Serge's painting?

Yvan No.

Marc Answer me this. You're getting married tomorrow and you and Catherine get this painting as a wedding present. Does it make you happy? . . .
Does it make you happy? . . .

Yvan, alone.

Yvan Of course it doesn't make me happy.
It doesn't make me happy, but, generally speaking, I'm not the sort of person who can say I'm happy, just like that.
I'm trying to . . . I'm trying to think of an occasion when I could have said yes, I'm happy . . . Are you happy to be getting married, my mother stupidly asked me one day, are you at least happy to be getting married? . . . Why wouldn't I be, Mother?

What do you mean, why wouldn't I be? You're either happy or you're not happy, what's 'Why wouldn't I be?' got to do with it? . . .

Serge, alone.

Serge As far as I'm concerned, it's not white.

When I say as far as I'm concerned, I mean objectively.

Objectively speaking, it's not white.

It has a white background, with a whole range of greys . . .

There's even some red in it.

You could say it's very pale.

I wouldn't like it if it was white.

Marc thinks it's white . . . that's his limit . . .

Marc thinks it's white because he's got hung up on the idea that it's white.

Unlike Yvan. Yvan can see it isn't white.

Marc can think what he likes, what do I care?

Marc, alone.

Marc Obviously I should have taken the Ignatia.

Why do I have to be so categorical?

What possible difference can it make to me if Serge lets himself be taken in by modern art?

I mean, it is a serious matter. But I could have found some other way to put it to him.

I could have taken a less aggressive tone.

Even if it makes me physically ill that my best friend has bought a white painting, all the same I ought to avoid attacking him about it.

I ought to be nice to him.

From now on, I'm on my best behaviour.

At Serge's.

Serge Feel like a laugh?

Marc Go on.

Serge Yvan liked the Antrios.

Marc Where is it? . . .

Serge You want another look?

Marc Fetch it out.

Serge I knew you'd come round to it! . . .

He exits and returns with the painting. A moment of contemplation.

Yvan got the hang of it. Right away.

Marc Mm.

Serge All right, listen, it's just a picture, we don't have to get bogged down with it, life's too short . . . By the way, have you read this? (*He picks up* De Vita Beata *by Seneca and throws it onto the low table just in front of Marc.*) Read it, it's a masterpiece.

Marc picks up the book, opens it and leafs through it.

Incredibly modern. Read that, you don't need to read anything else. What with the office, the hospital, Françoise, who's now decreed that I'm to see the children every weekend – which is something new for Françoise, the notion that children need a father – I don't have time to read any more, I'm obliged to go straight for the essentials.

Marc . . . As in painting. . . where you've ingeniously eliminated form and colour. Those old chestnuts.

Serge Yes . . . Although I'm still capable of appreciating more figurative work. Like your Flemish job. Very restful.

27

Marc What's Flemish about it? It's a view of Carcassonne.

Serge Yes, but I mean . . . it's slightly Flemish in style . . . the window, the view, the . . . in any case, it's very pretty.

Marc It's not worth anything, you know that.

Serge What difference does that make? . . . Anyway, in a few years God knows if the Antrios will be worth anything!

Marc . . . You know, I've been thinking. I've been thinking and I've changed my mind. The other day, driving across Paris, I was thinking about you and I said to myself: isn't there, deep down, something really poetic about what Serge has done? . . . Isn't surrendering to this incoherent urge to buy in fact an authentically poetic impulse?

Serge You're very conciliatory today. Unrecognisable. What's this bland, submissive tone of voice? It doesn't suit you at all, by the way.

Marc No, no, I'm trying to explain, I'm apologising.

Serge Apologising? What for?

Marc I'm too thin-skinned, I'm too highly strung, I over-react . . . You could say, I lack judgement.

Serge Read Seneca.

Marc That's it. See, for instance, you say, 'Read Seneca,' and I could easily have got annoyed. I'm quite capable of being really annoyed by your saying to me, in the course of our conversation, 'Read Seneca.' Which is absurd!

Serge No. It's not absurd.

Marc Really?

Serge No, because you thought you could identify . . .

Marc I didn't say I *was* annoyed . . .

Serge You said you could easily . . .

Marc Yes, yes. I could easily . . .

Serge . . . get annoyed, and I understand that. Because when I said, 'Read Seneca,' you thought you could identify a kind of superiority. You tell me you lack judgement and my answer is, 'Read Seneca,' well, it's obnoxious!

Marc It is, rather.

Serge Having said that, it's true you lack judgement, because I didn't say, 'Read Seneca,' I said, 'Read Seneca!'

Marc You're right. You're right.

Serge The fact of the matter is, you've quite simply lost your sense of humour.

Marc Probably.

Serge You've lost your sense of humour, Marc. You really have lost your sense of humour, old chap. When I was talking to Yvan the other day, we agreed you'd lost your sense of humour. Where the hell is he? He's incapable of being on time, it's infuriating! We'll miss the beginning!

Marc Yvan thinks I've lost my sense of humour? . . .

Serge Yvan agrees with me that recently you've somewhat lost your sense of humour.

Marc The last time you saw each other, Yvan said he liked your painting very much and I'd lost my sense of humour . . .

Serge Oh, yes, that, yes, the painting, really, very much. And he meant it . . . What's that you're eating?

Marc Ignatia.

Serge Oh, you believe in homeopathy now?

Marc I don't believe in anything.

Serge Didn't you think Yvan had lost a lot of weight?

Marc So's she.

Serge It's the wedding, eating away at them.

Marc Yes.

They laugh.

Serge How's Paula?

Marc All right. (*He indicates the Antrios.*) Where are you going to put it?

Serge Haven't decided. There. Or there? . . . Too ostentatious.

Marc Are you going to have it framed?

Serge laughs discreetly.

Serge No! . . . No, no . . .

Marc Why not?

Serge It's not supposed to be framed.

Marc Is that right?

Serge The artist doesn't want it to be. It mustn't be interrupted. It's already in its setting. (*He signals Marc over to examine the edge.*) Look . . . you see . . .

Marc What is it, Elastoplast?

Serge No, it's a kind of Kraft paper . . . Made up by the artist.

Marc It's funny, the way you say 'the artist'.

Serge What else am I supposed to say?

Marc You say 'the artist' when you could say 'the painter' or . . . whatever his name is . . . Antrios . . .

Serge So? . . .

Marc But you say 'the artist' as if he's a sort of . . . well, anyway, doesn't matter. What are we seeing? Let's try and see something with a bit of substance for once.

Serge It's eight o'clock. Everything will have started. I can't imagine how this man, who has nothing whatsoever to do – am I right? – manages to be late every single time. Where the fuck is he?

Marc Let's just have dinner.

Serge All right. It's five past eight. We said we'd meet between seven and half-past. . . What d'you mean, the way I say 'the artist'?

Marc Nothing. I was going to say something stupid.

Serge Well, go on.

Marc You say 'the artist' as if . . . as if he's some unattainable being. The artist . . . some sort of god . . .

Serge laughs.

Serge Well, for me, he is a god! You don't think I'd have forked out a fortune for a mere mortal! . . .

Marc I see.

Serge I went to the Pompidou on Monday. You know how many Antrioses they have at the Pompidou? Three! Three Antrioses! . . . At the Pompidou!

Marc Amazing.

Serge And mine's as good as any of them! If not better! . . .

31

Listen, I have a suggestion, let's give Yvan exactly three more minutes and then bugger off. I've found a very good new place. Lyonnaise.

Marc Why are you so jumpy?

Serge I'm not jumpy.

Marc Yes, you are jumpy.

Serge I am not jumpy – well, I am, I'm jumpy because this slackness is intolerable, this inability to practise any kind of self-discipline!

Marc The fact is, I'm getting on your nerves and you're taking it out on poor Yvan.

Serge What do you mean, 'poor Yvan', are you taking the piss? You're not getting on my nerves, why should you be getting on my nerves?

Serge He is getting on my nerves. It's true.
He's getting on my nerves.
It's this ingratiating tone of voice. A little smile behind every word.
It's as if he's forcing himself to be pleasant.
Don't be pleasant, whatever you do, don't be pleasant!
Could it be buying the Antrios? . . . Could buying the Antrios have triggered off this feeling of constraint between us?
Buying something . . . without his backing? . . .
Well, bugger his backing! Bugger your backing, Marc!

Marc Could it be the Antrios, buying the Antrios?
No –
It started some time ago . . .

32

To be precise, it started on the day we were discussing some work of art and you uttered, quite seriously, the word 'deconstruction'.

It wasn't so much the word 'deconstruction' which upset me, it was the air of solemnity you imbued it with.

You said, humourlessly, unapologetically, without a trace of irony, the word *deconstruction* – you, my friend.

I wasn't sure how best to deal with the situation, so I made this throwaway remark, I said I think I must be getting intolerant in my old age, and you answered, who do you think you are? What makes you so high and mighty? . . .

What gives you the right to set yourself apart, Serge answered, in the bloodiest possible way. And quite unexpectedly.

You're just Marc, what makes you think you're so special?

That day, I should have punched him in the mouth.

And when he was lying there on the ground, half-dead, I should have said to him, you're supposed to be my friend, what sort of a friend are you, Serge, if you don't think your friends are special?

At Serge's.
Marc and Serge, as we left them.

Marc Lyonnaise, did you say? Bit heavy, isn't it? Bit fatty, all those sausages . . . what do you think?

The doorbell rings.

Serge Twelve minutes past eight.

Serge goes to open the door to Yvan. Yvan walks into the room, already talking.

Yvan So, a crisis, insoluble problem, major crisis, both stepmothers want their names on the wedding invitation. Catherine adores her stepmother, who more or less brought her up, she wants her name on the invitation, she wants it, and her stepmother is not anticipating, which is understandable, since the mother is dead, not appearing next to Catherine's father, whereas my stepmother, whom I detest, it's out of the question her name should appear on the invitation, but my father won't have his name on it if hers isn't, unless Catherine's stepmother's is left off, which is completely unacceptable, I suggested none of the parents' names should be on it, after all we're not adolescents, we can announce our wedding and invite people ourselves, so Catherine screamed her head off, arguing that would be a slap in the face for her parents, who were paying through the nose for the reception, and particularly for her stepmother, who's gone to so much trouble when she isn't even her daughter, and I finally let myself be persuaded, totally against my better judgement, because she wore me down, I finally agreed that my stepmother, whom I detest, who's a complete bitch, will have her name on the invitation, so I telephoned my mother to warn her, Mother, I said, I've done everything I can to avoid this, but we have absolutely no choice, Yvonne's name has to be on the invitation, she said, if Yvonne's name is on the invitation, take mine off it, Mother, I said, please, I beg you, don't make things even more difficult, and she said, how dare you suggest my name is left to float around the card on its own, as if I was some abandoned woman, below Yvonne, who'll be clamped on to your father's surname, like a limpet? I said to her, Mother, I have friends waiting for me, I'm going to hang up and we'll discuss all this tomorrow after a good night's sleep, she said, why is it I'm always an afterthought, what are you talking about, Mother, you're not always an afterthought, of course

I am, and when you say don't make things even more
difficult, what you mean is, everything's already been
decided, everything's been organised without me,
everything's been cooked up behind my back, good old
Huguette, she'll agree to anything and all this, she said –
to put the old tin lid on it – in aid of an event, the
importance of which I'm having some trouble grasping,
Mother, I have friends waiting for me, that's right, there's
always something better to do, anything's more important
than I am, goodbye, and she hung up, Catherine, who
was next to me, but who hadn't heard her side of the
conversation, said, what did she say, I said, she doesn't
want her name on the invitation with Yvonne, which is
understandable, I'm not talking about that, what was it
she said about the wedding, nothing, you're lying, I'm
not, Cathy, I promise you, she just doesn't want her
name on the invitation with Yvonne, call her back and
tell her when your son's getting married, you rise above
your vanity, you could say the same thing to your
stepmother, that's got nothing to do with it, Catherine
shouted, it's me, I'm the one who's insisting her name's
on it, it's not her, poor thing, she's tact personified, if she
had any idea of the problem this is causing, she'd be
down on her knees, begging for her name to be taken
off the invitation, now call your mother, so I called her
again, by now I'm in shreds, Catherine's listening on
the extension, Yvan, my mother says, up to now you've
conducted your affairs in the most chaotic way
imaginable and just because, out of the blue, you've
decided to embark on matrimony, I find myself obliged
to spend all afternoon and evening with your father,
a man I haven't seen for seventeen years and to whom
I was not expecting to have to reveal my hip size and my
puffy cheeks, not to mention Yvonne, who incidentally,
I may tell you, according to Félix Perolari, has now
taken up bridge – my mother also plays bridge – I can

see none of this can be helped, but on the invitation, the one item everyone is going to receive and examine, I insist on making a solo appearance, Catherine, listening on the extension, shakes her head and screws up her face in disgust, Mother, I say, why are you so selfish? I'm not selfish, I'm not selfish, Yvan, you're not going to start as well, you're not going to be like Mme Roméro this morning and tell me I have a heart of stone, that everybody in our family has a heart of stone, that's what Mme Roméro said this morning when I refused to raise her wages – she's gone completely mad, by the way – to sixty francs an hour tax free, she had the gall to say everyone in the family had a heart of stone, when she knows very well about poor André's pacemaker, you haven't even bothered to drop him a line, yes, that's right, very funny, everything's a joke to you, it's not me who's the selfish one, Yvan, you've still got a lot to learn about life, off you go, my boy, go on, go on, go and see your precious friends . . .

Silence.

Serge Then what? . . .

Yvan Then nothing. Nothing's been resolved. I hung up. Mini-drama with Catherine. Cut short, because I was late.

Marc Why do you let yourself be buggered around by all these women?

Yvan Why do I let myself be buggered around? I don't know! They're all insane.

Serge You've lost weight.

Yvan Of course I have. Half a stone. Purely through stress.

Marc Read Seneca . . .

Yvan *De Vita Beata,* just what I need!
What's he suggest?

Marc It's a masterpiece.

Yvan Oh?

Serge He hasn't read it.

Yvan Oh.

Marc No, but Serge just told me it was a masterpiece.

Serge I said it was a masterpiece because it is a masterpiece.

Marc Quite.

Serge It is a masterpiece.

Marc Why are you getting annoyed?

Serge You seem to be insinuating I use the word masterpiece at the slightest excuse.

Marc Not at all . . .

Serge You said the word in a kind of sarcastic way . . .

Marc Not at all!

Serge Yes, yes, the word 'masterpiece' in a kind of . . .

Marc Is he crazy? Not at all! . . . However, when you used the word, you qualified it by saying 'incredibly modern'.

Serge Yes. So?

Marc You said 'incredibly modern', as if 'modern' was the highest compliment you could give. As if, when describing something, you couldn't think of anything more admirable, more profoundly admirable, than 'modern'.

Serge So?

Marc So nothing.
    And please note I made no mention of the word 'incredibly' . . . 'Incredibly modern'!

Serge You're really needling me today.

Marc No, I'm not . . .

Yvan You're not going to quarrel all evening, that would just about finish me!

Serge You don't think it's extraordinary that a man who wrote nearly two thousand years ago should still be bang up to date?

Marc No. Of course not. That's the definition of a classic.

Serge You're just playing with words.

Yvan So, what are we going to do? I suppose the cinema's up the spout, sorry. Shall we eat?

Marc Serge tells me you're very taken with his painting.

Yvan Yes . . . I am quite . . . taken with it, yes . . .
You're not, I gather.

Marc No.
Let's go and eat. Serge knows a tasty spot. Lyonnaise.

Serge You think the food's too fatty.

Marc I think the food's a bit on the fatty side, but I don't mind giving it a whirl.

Serge No, if you think the food's too fatty, we'll find somewhere else.

Marc No, I don't mind giving it a whirl.

Serge We'll go to the restaurant if you think you'll like it. If not, we won't.
(to Yvan) You like Lyonnaise food?

Yvan I'll do whatever you like.

Marc He'll do whatever you like. Whatever you like, he'll always do.

Yvan What's the matter with you? You're both behaving very strangely.

Serge He's right, you might once in a while have an opinion of your own.

Yvan Listen, if you think you're going to use me as a coconut shy, I'm out of here! I've put up with enough today.

Marc Where's your sense of humour, Yvan?

Yvan What?

Marc Where's your sense of humour, old chap?

Yvan Where's my sense of humour? I don't see anything to laugh at. Where's my sense of humour, are you trying to be funny?

Marc I think recently you've somewhat lost your sense of humour. You want to watch out, believe me!

Yvan What's the matter with you?

Marc Don't you think recently I've also somewhat lost my sense of humour?

Yvan Oh, I see!

Serge All right, that's enough, let's make a decision. Tell you the truth, I'm not even hungry.

Yvan You're both really sinister this evening.

Serge You want my opinion about your women problems?

Yvan Go on.

Serge In my view, the most hysterical of them all is Catherine. By far.

Marc No question.

Serge And if you're already letting yourself be buggered around by her, you're in for a hideous future.

Yvan What can I do?

Marc Cancel it.

Yvan Cancel the wedding?

Serge He's right.

Yvan But I can't, are you crazy?

Marc Why not?

Yvan Well, because I can't, that's all! It's all arranged. I've only been working at the stationery business for a month . . .

Marc What's that got to do with it?

Yvan It's her uncle's stationery business, he had absolutely no need to take on anyone, least of all someone who's only ever worked in textiles.

Serge You must do what you like. I've told you what I think.

Yvan I'm sorry, Serge, I don't mean to be rude, but you're not necessarily the person I'd come to for matrimonial advice. You can't claim to have been a great success in that field . . .

Serge Precisely.

Yvan I can't back out of the wedding. I know Catherine is hysterical, but she has her good points. There are certain crucial qualities you need when you're marrying someone like me . . . (*He indicates the Antrios.*) Where are you going to put it?

Serge I don't know yet.

Yvan Why don't you put it there?

Serge Because there, it'd be wiped out by the sunlight.

Yvan Oh, yes.
   I thought of you today at the shop, we ran off five hundred posters by this bloke who paints white flowers, totally white, on a white background.

Serge The Antrios is not white.

Yvan No, of course not. I was just saying.

Marc You think this painting is not white, Yvan?

Yvan Not entirely, no . . .

Marc Ah. Then what colour is it?

Yvan Various colours . . . There's yellow, there's grey, some slightly ochrish lines.

Marc And you're moved by these colours?

Yvan Yes . . . I'm moved by these colours.

Marc You have no substance, Yvan. You're flabby, you're an amoeba.

Serge Why are you attacking Yvan like this?

Marc Because he's a little arse-licker, he's obsequious, dazzled by money, dazzled by what he believes to be culture, and as you know culture is something I absolutely piss on.

   Brief silence.

Serge . . . What's got into you?

Marc (*to Yvan*) How could you, Yvan? . . . And in front of me. In front of me, Yvan?

Yvan What d'you mean, 'in front of you'? . . . What d'you mean, 'in front of you'?

I find these colours touching. Yes. If it's all the same to you.

Stop wanting to control everything.

Marc How could you say, in front of me, that you find these colours touching?

Yvan Because it's the truth.

Marc The truth? You find these colours touching?

Yvan Yes. I find these colours touching.

Marc You find these colours touching, Yvan?!

Serge He finds these colours touching! He's perfectly entitled to!

Marc No, he's not entitled to.

Serge What do you mean, he's not entitled to?

Marc He's not entitled to.

Yvan I'm not entitled to? . . .

Marc No.

Serge Why is he not entitled to? I don't think you're very well. Perhaps you ought to go and see someone.

Marc He's not entitled to say he finds these colours touching, because he doesn't.

Yvan I don't find these colours touching?

Marc There are no colours. You can't see them. And you don't find them touching.

Yvan Speak for yourself!

Marc This is really demeaning, Yvan! . . .

Serge Who do you think you are, Marc? . . .

Who are you to legislate? You don't like anything, you despise everyone. You take pride in not being a man of your time . . .

Marc What's that supposed to mean, 'a man of my time'?

Yvan Right. I'm off.

Serge Where are you going?

Yvan I'm off. I don't see why I have to put up with your tantrums.

Serge Don't go! You're not going to start taking offence, are you? . . . If you go, you're giving in to him.

Yvan stands there, hesitating, caught between two possibilities.

A man of his time is a man who lives in his own time.

Marc Balls. How can a man live in any other time but his own? Answer me that.

Serge A man of his time is someone of whom it can be said in twenty years' or in a hundred years' time, he was representative of his era.

Marc Hm.
To what end?

Serge What do you mean, 'to what end'?

Marc What use is it to me if one day somebody says, I was representative of my era?

Serge Listen, old fruit, we're not talking about you, if you can imagine such a thing! We don't give a fuck about you! A man of his time, I'm trying to explain to you, like most people you admire, is someone who makes some contribution to the human race . . . A man

43

of his time doesn't assume the history of art has come to an end with a pseudo-Flemish view of Cavaillon . . .

Marc Carcassonne.

Serge Same thing. A man of his time plays his part in the fundamental dynamic of evolution . . .

Marc And that's a good thing, in your view?

Serge It's not good or bad – why do you always have to moralise? It's just the way things are.

Marc And you, for example, you play your part in the fundamental dynamic of evolution.

Serge I do.

Marc What about Yvan? . . .

Yvan Surely not. What sort of part can an amoeba play?

Serge In his way, Yvan is a man of his time.

Marc How can you tell? Not from that daub hanging over his mantelpiece!

Yvan That is not a daub!

Serge It is a daub.

Yvan It is not!

Serge What's the difference? Yvan represents a certain way of life, a way of thinking which is completely modern. And so do you. I'm sorry, but you're a typical man of your time. And in fact the harder you try not to be, the more you are.

Marc Well, that's all right then. So what's the problem?

Serge There's no problem, except for you, because you take pride in your desire to shut yourself off from humanity. And you'll never manage it. It's like you're in a quicksand, the more you struggle to get out of it, the deeper you sink. Now apologise to Yvan.

Marc Yvan is a coward.

At this point, Yvan makes his decision, and exits in a rush.
Slight pause.

Serge Well done.

Silence.

Marc It wasn't a good idea to meet this evening . . . was it? . . . I'd better go as well . . .

Serge Maybe . . .

Marc Right.

Serge You're the coward . . . attacking someone who's incapable of defending himself . . . as you well know.

Marc You're right . . . you're right and when you put it like that, it makes me feel even worse . . . the thing is, all of a sudden, I can't understand, I have no idea what Yvan and I have in common . . . I have no idea what my relationship with him consists of.

Serge Yvan's always been as he is.

Marc No. He used to be eccentric, kind of absurd . . . he was always unstable, but his eccentricity was disarming . . .

Serge What about me?

Marc What about you?

Serge Have you any idea what you and I have in common? . . .

Marc That's a question that could take us down a very long road . . .

Serge Lead on.

Short silence.

Marc . . . I'm sorry I upset Yvan.

Serge Ah! At last you've said something approximately human . . . What makes it worse is that the daub he has hanging over his mantelpiece was I'm afraid painted by his father.

Marc Was it? Shit.

Serge Yes . . .

Marc But you said . . .

Serge Yes, yes, but I remembered as soon as I'd said it.

Marc Oh, shit . . .

Serge Mm . . .

Slight pause.
   The doorbell rings. Serge goes to answer it. Yvan enters immediately, talking as he arrives, as before.

Yvan Yvan returns! The lift was full, I plunged off down the stairs, clattering all the way down, thinking, a coward, an amoeba, no substance, I thought I'll come back with a gun and blow his head off, then he'll see how flabby and obsequious I am, I got to the ground floor and I said to myself, listen, mate, you haven't been in therapy for six years to finish up shooting your best friend and you haven't been in therapy for six years without learning that some deep malaise must lie behind his insane aggression, so I relaunch myself, telling myself as I mount the penitential stair, this is a cry for help. I have to help Marc if it's the last thing I do . . . In fact the other day I discussed you both with Finkelzohn . . .

Serge You discussed us with Finkelzohn?

46

Yvan I discuss everything with Finkelzohn.

Serge And why exactly were you discussing us?

Marc I forbid you to discuss me with that arsehole.

Yvan You're in no position to forbid me anything.

Serge Why were you discussing us?

Yvan I knew your relationship was under strain and I wanted Finkelzohn to explain . . .

Serge And what did the bastard say?

Yvan He said something rather amusing . . .

Marc They're allowed to give their opinions?

Yvan No, they never give their opinions, but this time he did give his opinion, he even made a gesture and he never makes a gesture, he's always rigid, I sometimes say to him, for God's sake, move about a bit!

Serge All right, what did he say?

Marc Who gives a fuck what he said?

Serge What did he say?

Marc What possible interest could we have in what he said?

Serge I want to know what the bastard said, all right? Shit!

Yvan reaches into his jacket pocket.

Yvan You want to know? . . .

He fetches out a piece of folded paper.

Marc You took notes?

Yvan (*unfolding it*) I wrote it down because it was complicated . . . Shall I read it to you?

Serge Go on.

Yvan . . . 'If I'm who I am because I'm who I am and you're who you are because you're who you are, then I'm who I am and you're who you are. If, on the other hand, I'm who I am because you're who you are, and if you're who you are because I'm who I am, then I'm not who I am and you're not who you are . . .'

You see why I had to write it down.

Short silence.

Marc How much do you pay this man?

Yvan Four hundred francs a session, twice a week.

Marc Great.

Serge And in cash. I found something out, they don't allow you to pay by cheque. Freud said you have to feel the banknotes as they slip through your fingers.

Marc What a lucky man you are, to be getting the benefit of this fellow's experience.

Serge Absolutely! . . . We'd really appreciate it if you'd copy that out for us.

Marc Yes. It's bound to come in handy.

Yvan carefully refolds the piece of paper.

Yvan You're wrong. It's very profound.

Marc If it's because of him you've come back to turn the other cheek, you should be grateful to him. He's turned you into a pudding, but you're happy, that's all that counts.

Yvan (*to Serge*) And all this because he doesn't want to believe I like your Antrios.

Serge I don't give a fuck what you think of it. Either of you.

Yvan The more I see it, the more I like it, honestly.

Serge Let's stop talking about the painting, shall we, once and for all. I have no interest in discussing it further.

Marc Why are you so touchy?

Serge I am not touchy, Marc. You've told us what you think. Fine. The subject is closed.

Marc You're getting upset.

Serge I am not getting upset. I'm exhausted.

Marc See, if you're touchy about it, it means you're too caught up in other people's opinions . . .

Serge I'm exhausted, Marc. This is completely pointless . . . To tell you the truth, I'm quite close to getting bored with the pair of you.

Yvan Let's go and eat.

Serge You go, why don't you go off together?

Yvan No! It's so rare the three of us are together.

Serge Just as well, by the look of it.

Yvan I don't understand what's going on. Can't we just calm down? There's no reason to insult each other, especially over a painting.

Serge You realise all this 'calm down' and behaving like the vicar is just adding fuel to the fire! Is this something new?

Yvan I will not be undermined.

Marc This is most impressive. Perhaps I should go to Finkelzohn! . . .

Yvan You can't. There are no vacancies.
   What's that you're eating?

49

Marc Gelsemium.

Yvan I've given in to the logic of events, marriage, children, death. Stationery. What can go wrong?

Moved by a sudden impulse, Serge picks up the Antrios and takes it back where he found it, in the next room. He returns immediately.

Marc We're not worthy to look at it . . .

Serge Exactly.

Marc Or are you afraid, if it stays in my presence, you'll finish up looking at it through my eyes?

Serge No. You know what Paul Valéry says? And I'd go quite a bit further.

Marc I don't give a fuck what Paul Valéry says.

Serge You've gone off Paul Valéry?

Marc Don't quote Paul Valéry at me.

Serge But you used to love Paul Valéry.

Marc I don't give a fuck what Paul Valéry says.

Serge But I discovered him through you. You're the one who put me on to Paul Valéry.

Marc Don't quote Paul Valéry at me, I don't give a fuck what Paul Valéry says.

Serge What do you give a fuck about?

Marc I give a fuck about you buying that painting.
    I give a fuck about you spending two hundred grand on that piece of shit.

Yvan Don't start again, Marc!

Serge I'm going to tell you what I give a fuck about – since everyone is coming clean – I give a fuck about your sniggering and insinuations, your suggestion that I also think this picture is a grotesque joke. You've denied that I could feel a genuine attachment to it. You've tried to set up some kind of loathsome complicity between us. And that's what's made me feel, Marc, to repeat your expression, that we have less and less in common recently, your perpetual display of suspicion.

Marc It's true I can't imagine you genuinely loving that painting.

Yvan But why?

Marc Because I love Serge and I can't love the Serge who's capable of buying that painting.

Serge Why do you say, 'buying', why don't you say, 'loving'?

Marc Because I can't say 'loving', I can't believe 'loving'.

Serge So why would I buy it, if I didn't love it?

Marc That's the nub of the question.

Serge (*to Yvan*) See how smug he is! All I'm doing is teasing him, and his answer is this serenely pompous heavy hint! . . . (*to Marc*) And it never crossed your mind for a second, however improbable it might seem, that I might really love it and that your vicious, inflexible opinions and your disgusting assumption of complicity might be hurtful to me?

Marc No.

Serge When you asked me what I thought of Paula – a girl who once spent an entire dinner party maintaining Elhers Danlos's syndrome could be cured homeopathically – did I say I found her ugly, repellent and charmless? I could have done.

YASMINA REZA

Marc Is that what you think of Paula?

Serge What's your theory?

Yvan No, of course he doesn't think that! You couldn't possibly think that of Paula!

Marc Answer me.

Serge You see the effect you can have!

Marc Do you think what you just said about Paula?

Serge Worse, actually.

Yvan No!

Marc Worse, Serge? Worse than repellent? Will you explain how someone can be worse than repellent?

Serge Aha! When it's something that concerns you personally, I see words can bite a little deeper!

Marc Serge, will you explain how someone can be worse than repellent . . .

Serge No need to take that frosty tone. Perhaps it's – let me try and answer you – perhaps it's the way she waves away cigarette smoke.

Marc The way she waves away cigarette smoke . . .

Serge Yes. The way she waves away cigarette smoke. What appears to you a gesture of no significance, what you think of as a harmless gesture is in fact the opposite, and the way she waves away cigarette smoke sits right at the heart of her repellentness.

Marc You're speaking to me of Paula, the woman who shares my life, in these intolerable terms, because you disapprove of her method of waving away cigarette smoke?

Serge That's right. Her method of waving away cigarette smoke condemns her out of hand.

Marc Serge, before I completely lose control, you'd better explain yourself. This is very serious, what you're doing.

Serge A normal woman would say, I'm sorry, I find the smoke a bit uncomfortable, would you mind moving your ashtray, but not her, she doesn't deign to speak, she describes her contempt in the air with this calculated gesture, wearily malicious, this hand movement she imagines is imperceptible, the implication of which is to say, go on, smoke, smoke, it's pathetic but what's the point of calling attention to it, which means you can't tell if it's you or your cigarette that's getting up her nose.

Yvan You're exaggerating!

Serge You notice he doesn't say I'm wrong, he says I'm exaggerating, but he doesn't say I'm wrong. Her method of waving away cigarette smoke reveals a cold, condescending and narrow-minded nature. Just what you're in the process of acquiring yourself. It's a shame, Marc, it's a real shame you've taken up with such a life-denying woman . . .

Yvan Paula is not life-denying! . . .

Marc Take back everything you've just said, Serge.

Serge No.

Yvan Yes, you must!

Marc Take back what you've just said . . .

Yvan Take it back, take it back! This is ridiculous!

Marc Serge, for the last time, I demand you take back what you've just said.

53

Serge In my view, the two of you are an aberration. A pair of fossils.

Marc throws himself at Serge. Yvan rushes forward to get between them.

Marc (*to Yvan*) Get off! . . .

Serge (*to Yvan*) Mind your own business!

A kind of bizarre struggle ensues, very short, which ends with a blow mistakenly landing on Yvan.

Yvan Oh, shit! . . . Oh, shit! . . .

Serge Show me, show me . . .

Yvan is groaning. More than is necessary, it would seem.

Come on, show me! . . . That's all right . . . it's nothing . . . Wait a minute . . .

He goes out and comes back with a compress.

There you are, hold that on it for a while.

Yvan . . . You're complete freaks, both of you. Two normal men gone completely insane!

Serge Don't get excited.

Yvan That really hurt! . . . If I find out you've burst my eardrum!

Serge Of course not.

Yvan How do you know? You're not ear, nose and throat! . . . Two old friends, educated people! . . .

Serge Go on, calm down.

Yvan You can't demolish someone because you don't like her method of waving away cigarette smoke!

Serge Yes, you can.

54

Yvan But it doesn't make any sense!

Serge What do you know about sense?

Yvan That's right, attack me, keep attacking me! . . .
I could be haemorrhaging internally, I've just seen a mouse
running past!

Serge It's a rat.

Yvan A rat?

Serge He comes and goes.

Yvan You have a rat?!

Serge Don't take the compress away, leave it where it is.

Yvan What's the matter with you? . . . What's happened
between you? Something must have happened for you to
go this demented.

Serge I've bought a work of art which makes Marc
uncomfortable.

Yvan You're starting again! . . . You're in a downward
spiral, both of you, you can't stop yourselves . . . It's like
me and Yvonne. The most pathological relationship you
can imagine!

Serge Who's Yvonne?

Yvan My stepmother!

Serge It's a long time since you mentioned her.

Brief silence.

Marc Why didn't you tell me right away what you
thought about Paula?

Serge I didn't want to upset you.

Marc No, no, no . . .

55

Serge What do you mean, 'no, no, no'?

Marc No.
  When I asked you what you thought of Paula, what you said was: she's a perfect match for you.

Serge Yes . . .

Marc Which sounded quite positive, coming from you.

Serge Sure . . .

Marc Given the state you were in at the time.

Serge All right, what are you trying to prove?

Marc But today, your assessment of Paula, or in other words me, is far harsher.

Serge . . . I don't understand.

Marc Of course you understand.

Serge I don't.

Marc Since I can no longer support you in your frenzied, though recent, craving for novelty, I've become 'condescending', 'narrow-minded'. . . 'fossilised' . . .

Yvan I'm in agony! It's like a corkscrew drilling through my brain!

Serge Have a drop of brandy.

Yvan What do you think? . . . If something's shaken loose in my brain, don't you think alcohol's a bit of a risk?

Serge Would you like an aspirin?

Yvan I'm not sure aspirin agrees with me . . .

Serge Then what the hell do you want?

Yvan Don't worry about me. Carry on with your preposterous conversation, don't pay any attention to me.

Marc Easier said than done.

Yvan You might squeeze out a drop of compassion. But no.

Serge I don't mind your spending time with Paula. I don't resent you being with Paula.

Marc You've no reason to resent it.

Serge But you . . . you resent me . . . well, I was about to say, for being with the Antrios!

Marc Yes!

Serge I'm missing something here.

Marc I didn't replace you with Paula.

Serge Are you saying, I replaced you with the Antrios?

Marc Yes.

Serge . . . I replaced you with the Antrios?

Marc Yes. With the Antrios . . . and all it implies.

Serge (*to Yvan*) Do you understand what he's talking about?

Yvan I couldn't care less, you're both insane.

Marc In my time, you'd never have bought that picture.

Serge What's that supposed to mean, 'in your time'?

Marc The time you made a distinction between me and other people, when you judged things by my standards.

Serge Was there such a time?

Marc That's just cruel. And petty.

Serge No, I assure you, I'm staggered.

57

Marc And if Yvan hadn't turned into such a sponge, he'd back me up.

Yvan Go on, that's right, I've told you, it's water off a duck's back.

Marc (*to Serge*) There was a time you were proud to be my friend . . . You congratulated yourself on my peculiarity, on my taste for standing apart. You enjoyed exhibiting me untamed to your circle – you, whose life was so normal. I was your alibi. But . . . eventually, I suppose, that sort of affection dries up . . . Belatedly, you claim your independence.

Serge 'Belatedly' is nice.

Marc But I detest your independence. Its violence. You've abandoned me. I've been betrayed. As far as I'm concerned, you're a traitor.

Silence.

Serge (*to Yvan*) . . . If I understand correctly, he was my mentor!

Yvan doesn't respond.
Marc stares at him contemptuously.
Slight pause.

. . . And if I loved you as my mentor . . . what was the nature of your feelings?

Marc You can guess.

Serge Yes, yes, but I want to hear you say it.

Marc . . . I enjoyed your admiration. I was flattered. I was always grateful to you for thinking of me as a man apart. I even thought being a man apart was a somehow superior condition, until one day you pointed out to me that it wasn't.

58

Serge This is very alarming.

Marc It's the truth.

Serge What a disaster . . .!

Marc Yes, what a disaster!

Serge What a disaster!

Marc Especially for me . . . Whereas you've found a new family. Your penchant for idolatry has unearthed new objects of worship. The Artist! . . . *Deconstruction!*

  Short silence.

Yvan What is deconstruction? . . .

Marc You don't know about deconstruction? . . . Ask Serge, he's very much on top of the subject . . . (to *Serge*) To convince me some ridiculous artwork is comprehensible, you pick a phrase from *Builders' Weekly* . . . Oh, you're smiling! You see, when you smile like that, I think there's still some hope, like an idiot . . .

Yvan Why don't you make up? And let's spend an enjoyable evening, all this is ludicrous!

Marc . . . It's my fault. We haven't seen much of one another recently. I've been away and you started mixing with the great and the good . . . the Ropses . . . the Desprez-Couderts . . . that dentist, Guy Hallié . . . he's the one who . . .

Serge No, no, no, no, not at all, he's from another world, he only likes conceptual Art . . .

Marc It's all the same thing.

Serge No, it's not all the same thing.

Marc You see, more evidence of how I let you slip away . . . now when we talk we can't even make ourselves understood.

Serge I had no idea whatsoever – really, it's come as a complete surprise – the extent to which I was under your influence and in your control.

Marc Not in my control, as it turns out . . . You should never leave your friends unchaperoned. Your friends need to be chaperoned, otherwise they'll get away . . .

Look at poor Yvan, whose chaotic behaviour used to delight us, we've allowed him to become this timid stationer . . . Practically married . . . He brought us his originality and now he's making every effort to piss it away.

Serge Us! He brought us! Do you realise what you're saying? Everything has to revolve around you! Why can't you learn to love people for themselves, Marc?

Marc What does that mean, 'for themselves'?

Serge For what they are.

Marc But what are they?! What are they?! . . .

Apart from my faith in them? . . .

I'm desperate to find a friend who has some kind of prior existence. So far, I've had no luck. I've had to mould you . . . But you see, it never works. There comes a day when your creature has dinner with the Desprez-Couderts and, to confirm his new status, goes off and buys a white painting.

Silence.

Serge So here we are at the end of a fifteen-year friendship . . .

Marc Yes . . .

Yvan Pathetic . . .

Marc You see, if we'd only managed to have a normal discussion, that is, if I'd been able to put my point of view without losing my temper . . .

Serge Well? . . .

Marc Nothing . . .

Serge Yes. Go on. Why can't we exchange one single dispassionate word?

Marc . . . I don't believe in the values which dominate contemporary art. The rule of novelty. The rule of surprise.
  Surprise is dead meat, Serge. No sooner conceived than dead.

Serge All right. So?

Marc That's all.
  Except that my appeal to you has always been my surprise value.

Serge What are you talking about?

Marc A surprise which has lasted quite some time, I'll admit.

Yvan Finkelzohn is a genius.
  I told you he'd understood the whole thing!

Marc I'd prefer it if you stopped refereeing, Yvan, and stopped imagining you're not fully implicated in this conversation.

Yvan You want to implicate me, I refuse, what's it to do with me? I've already got a burst eardrum, you work things out for yourselves!

Marc Perhaps he does have a burst eardrum. I hit him very hard.

  Serge sniggers.

Serge Please, stop boasting.

Marc See, Yvan, what I can't bear about you at the moment – quite apart from what I've already told you –

YASMINA REZA

is your urge to put Serge and me on the same level. You
would like us to be equal. To indulge your cowardice.
Talking on an equal footing, equal the way you thought
of us when we were friends. But we never were equal,
Yvan. You have to choose.

Yvan I have chosen.

Marc Excellent.

Serge I don't need a supporter.

Marc You're not going to turn the poor boy down?

Yvan Why do we see each other, if we hate each other?
It's obvious we do hate each other! Or rather, I don't
hate you, but you hate each other! And you hate me! So
why do we see each other? . . . I was looking forward to
a relaxing evening after a ridiculously fraught week,
meeting my two best friends, going to the cinema, having
a laugh, getting away from all these dramas . . .

Serge Are you aware that you've talked about nothing
but yourself?

Yvan Well, who are you talking about? Everybody talks
about themselves!

Serge You fuck up our evening, you . . .

Yvan I fuck up your evening?! . . .

Serge Yes.

Yvan I fuck up your evening?! I?! I fuck up your
evening?!

Marc All right, don't get excited!

Yvan You're saying it's me who's fucked up your
evening?! . . .

Serge How many more times are you going to say it?

Yvan Just answer the question, are you saying it's me who's fucked up your evening?! . . .

Marc You arrive three-quarters of an hour late, you don't apologise, you deluge us with your domestic woes . . .

Serge And your inertia, your sheer neutral spectator's inertia has lured Marc and me into the worst excesses.

Yvan You as well! You're starting as well?

Serge Yes, because on this subject I'm entirely in agreement with him. You create the conditions of conflict.

Marc You've been piping up with this finicky, subservient voice of reason ever since you arrived, it's intolerable.

Yvan You know I could burst into tears . . . I could start crying right now . . . I'm very close to tears.

Marc Cry.

Serge Cry.

Yvan Cry! You're telling me to cry!

Marc You've every reason to cry, you're marrying a gorgon, you're losing your two best friends . . .

Yvan That's it then, is it, it's all over!

Marc You said it yourself, what's the point of seeing each other if we hate each other?

Yvan What about my wedding?! You're my witnesses, remember?

Serge Find someone else.

Yvan I can't! You're on the invitation!

Marc You can choose someone else at the last minute.

Yvan You're not allowed to!

Serge Of course you are!

Yvan You're not!

Marc Don't panic, we'll come.

Serge But what you ought to do is cancel the wedding.

Marc He's right.

Yvan Oh, shit! What have I ever done to you? Shit!

He bursts into tears. Time passes.

It's brutal what you're doing! You could have had your fight after the twelfth, but no, you're determined to ruin my wedding, a wedding which is already a catastrophe, which has made me lose half a stone, and now you're completely buggering it up! The only two people whose presence guaranteed some spark of satisfaction are determined to destroy one another – just my luck! . . . (*to Marc*) You think I like packs of filofax paper or rolls of Sellotape, you think any normal man wakes up one day desperate to sell expandable document wallets? . . . What am I supposed to do? I pissed around for forty years, I made you laugh, oh, yes, wonderful, I made all my friends laugh their heads off playing the fool, but come the evening, who was left solitary as a rat? Who crawled back into his hole every evening all on his own? This buffoon, dying of loneliness, who'd switch on anything that talks, and who does he find on the answering machine? His mother. His mother. And his mother.

A short silence.

Marc Don't get yourself in such a state.

Yvan Don't get yourself in such a state! Who got me in this state in the first place? Look at me – I don't have your refined sensibilities. I'm a lightweight. I have no opinions.

Marc Calm down . . .

Yvan Don't tell me to calm down! What possible reason do I have to calm down, are you trying to drive me demented, telling me to calm down? Calm down's the worst thing you can say to someone who's lost his calm! I'm not like you, I don't want to be an authority figure, I don't want to be a point of reference, I don't want to be self-sufficient, I just want to be your friend Yvan the joker! Yvan the joker!

Silence.

Serge Could we try to steer clear of pathos? . . .

Yvan I've finished.
Haven't you got any nibbles? Anything, just to stop me from passing out.

Serge I have some olives.

Yvan Hand them over.

Serge reaches for a little bowl of olives and hands it to him.

Serge (*to Marc*) Want some?

Marc nods. Yvan hands him the bowl. They eat olives.

Yvan Is there somewhere to put the . . .

Serge Yes.

He fetches a saucer and puts it on the table.
Pause.

Yvan (*still eating olives*) . . . To think we've reached these extremes . . . Apocalypse because of a white square . . .

Serge It is not white.

Yvan A piece of white shit! . . .

He's seized by uncontrollable laughter.

That's what it is, a piece of white shit! . . . Let's face it, mate . . . What you've bought is insane! . . .

Marc laughs, caught up by Yvan's extravagance. Serge leaves the room. He returns immediately with the Antrios.

Serge Do you have one of your famous felt-tips? . . .

Yvan What for? . . . You're not going to draw on the painting.

Serge Do you or don't you?

Yvan Just a minute . . . (*He goes through the pockets of his jacket.*) Yes . . . A blue one . . .

Serge Give it to me.

Yvan hands the felt-tip to Serge.
Serge takes the felt-tip, pulls the top off it, examines the tip for a moment, puts the top back on.
He looks up at Marc and throws him the felt-tip.
Marc catches it.
Slight pause.

(*to Marc*) Go on.

Silence.

Go on!

Marc approaches the painting . . .
He looks at Serge . . .
Then he takes the top off the felt-tip.

Yvan You're not going to do it! . . .

Marc is looking at Serge.

Serge Come on.

Yvan You're raving mad, both of you!

Marc leans towards the painting.
   Under Yvan's horrified gaze, he draws the felt-tip along one of the diagonal scars. Serge remains impassive.
   Then, carefully, on this slope, Marc draws a little skier with a woolly hat.
   When he's finished, he straightens up and contemplates his work.
   Serge remains adamantine.
   Yvan is as if turned to stone.
   Silence.

Serge Well, I'm starving.
   Shall we eat?

Marc tries a smile. He puts the top back on and playfully throws the pen to Yvan, who catches it.

At Serge's.
   At the back, hanging on the wall, the Antrios.
Standing in front of the canvas, Marc is holding a basin of water, into which Serge is dipping a little piece of cloth. Marc has rolled up his sleeves and Serge is wearing a little builder's apron which is too short for him. Round about are various cleaning products, bottles of white spirit and stain remover, rags and sponges. Moving very delicately, Serge puts the finishing touch to the cleaning of the painting.
   The Antrios is as white as ever. Marc puts down the basin and looks at the painting. Serge turns to Yvan, who's sitting off to one side. Yvan nods approvingly. Serge steps back and contemplates the picture in his turn.
   Silence.

Yvan *(as if alone, speaking in a slightly muffled voice)* . . .
The day after the wedding, at the Montparnasse

cemetery, Catherine put her wedding bouquet and a little
bag of sugared almonds on her mother's grave. I slipped
away to cry behind a monument and in the evening,
thinking again about this touching tribute, I started
silently sobbing in my bed. I absolutely must speak to
Finkelzohn about my tendency to cry, I cry all the time,
it's not normal for someone my age. It started, or at least
clearly revealed itself at Serge's, the evening of the white
painting. After Serge, in an act of pure madness, had
demonstrated to Marc that he cared more about him
than he did about his painting, we went and had dinner,
chez Emile. Over dinner, Serge and Marc took the
decision to try to rebuild a relationship destroyed by
word and deed. At a certain moment, one of them used
the expression 'trial period' and I burst into tears.

This expression, 'trial period', applied to our friendship,
set off in me an uncontrollable and ridiculous convulsion.

In fact I can no longer bear any kind of rational
argument, nothing formative in the world, nothing great
or beautiful in the world has ever been born of rational
argument.

Pause.
Serge dries his hands. He goes to empty the basin
of water then puts away all the cleaning products,
until there's no sign left of domestic activity. Once
again he looks at his painting. Then he turns and
advances towards the audience.

Serge When Marc and I succeeded in obliterating the
skier, with the aid of Swiss soap with added ox gall,
recommended by Paula, I looked at the Antrios and
turned to Marc:
'Did you know ink from felt-tips was washable?'
'No,' Marc said . . . 'No . . . did you?'
'No,' I said, very fast, lying. I came within an inch of
saying, yes, I did know. But how could I have launched

our trial period with such a disappointing admission? On the other hand, was it right to start with a lie? . . . A lie! Let's be reasonable. Why am I so absurdly virtuous? Why does my relationship with Marc have to be so complicated? . . .

Gradually, the light begins to narrow down on the Antrios. Marc approaches the painting.

Marc Under the white clouds, the snow is falling.
You can't see the white clouds, or the snow.
Or the cold, or the white glow of the earth.
A solitary man glides downhill on his skis.
The snow is falling.
It falls until the man disappears back into the landscape.
My friend Serge, who's one of my oldest friends, has bought a painting.
It's a canvas about five foot by four.
It represents a man who moves across a space and disappears.

THE UNEXPECTED MAN

The Unexpected Man in this translation was first
performed by the Royal Shakespeare Company at
The Pit, Barbican Centre, London, on 8 April 1998.
The cast was as follows:

The Woman Eileen Atkins
The Man Michael Gambon

Director Matthew Warchus
Designer Mark Thompson
Lighting Designer Hugh Vanstone
Composer Gary Yershon
Sound Mic Pool

Characters

The Man

The Woman

A train compartment.
A man and a woman.
Both of them self-contained.
Nothing realistic. Air. Space.

A deliberate absence of stage directions.
Similarly (except at the end) the necessary silences
and pauses are not indicated in the text.

Each of them self-contained.

The Man Bitter.

It's all so bitter.

The curl of my lip is bitter.

Time, things, the inanimate objects I've stacked up around me, all of which have outlived their purpose, all of which are bitter.

There's nothing to be said for objects.

My friend Yuri has a Japanese girlfriend.

Totally flat-chested.

He's sixty-eight with a three-ounce prostate, she's forty and flat-chested.

It's all so bitter. The night is bitter.

Night. No love, no closeness, drifting in and out of sleep . . .

Jean told me someone or other had written a beautiful piece on insomnia. Arsehole. Last night I woke up at five needing to shit. It's all his fault. He vetoed my All Bran. Consequently, I have to shit at five o'clock in the morning. Stupid idiot's completely sabotaged my rhythms.

What good's it to me if someone or other writes a piece about insomnia!

Yuri, now he sleeps. He's always been able to sleep.

When I can't sleep I think of Yuri, fast asleep after parsimoniously depositing a little semen in his Japanese piggy bank.

Sleeping with women is bitter.

I can't stay in bed with a woman. With certain exceptions. The black girl at the Plaza, for example.

There was some sort of contact with the black girl, it more or less worked.

Not the sex, but the closeness, the rub of the flesh.

The more elementary the woman, the more comfortable I feel in bed. The cruder she is. The less she interests me in life, the better I feel in bed.

Animals rubbing together, nothing else is left.

The basic question is, wouldn't I in fact be better off sleeping with an animal?

Sex is bitter.

Bitter, always has been.

No question of a biography.

Absolutely – absolutely no question of a biography after I'm dead. That's what I have to say to that lawyer.

The biography of a writer, absolutely ridiculous.

Who knows the first thing about anybody's life?

Who can say anything remotely coherent about anybody else's life?

Who can say anything remotely coherent about life in general?

Did I write what I wanted to write? No, never.

I wrote what I was capable of writing, not what I wanted to.

All you ever do is what you're capable of.

How can your complete works, your contribution added to the world – and by the way, all the great laws of nature work on the principle of subtraction – how can your complete works be anything more than a mishmash of approximations, of constantly shifting boundaries?

Isn't the end result inevitable failure?

Only anonymous writing can hope to avoid failure.

All those idiots discussing their intentions.

All those idiots shovelling out opinions, not one of them who'll admit the whole thing's slipped away, the material's uncontrollable, I can't remember the original idea and all that's left is what came limping into port.

All those poor buggers assessing their contribution to

the world with furrowed brow, the great providers of opinions who turn up on the books programmes.

And you're not one of them, I suppose?

No.

What do you mean, no?

No. I've never appeared on a books programme.

Never gone near a books programme.

Only because you're a snob, old boy. You've done enough other things.

Lectures, you've given. Interviews, God knows how many!

Innumerable functions in your honour.

And as for the knitted brow, no need to worry.

Yours certainly is.

Now, this minute, your brow is furrowed.

Maurice Negear is crazy about his daughter.

She came forty-seventh out of eighty-three in the Yvelines Challenge Cup.

She's a big girl. I thought jockeys were supposed to be midgets.

The Yvelines Challenge Cup . . .

What should I do? How should I proceed?

What should I do –

See him?

Follow Jean's advice and just turn up?

Have a coffee in town as if nothing's happened? Talk about the weather?

If she says he's fifty-one, he's probably twice that.

On the other hand, I can't go on ignoring him, that would definitely be a mistake.

I mean, for Christ's sake, a father has a right to object to his daughter marrying a man with one foot in the grave!

Jean says he's very nice, quite interesting even, except you can't hear what he's saying.

An inaudible voice, and our family's been stentorian for generations.

You can't have a son-in-law with an inaudible voice. Sooner or later inaudibility will provoke you to the worst excesses.

Oh, Nathalie, why couldn't you have been mad on horses like Maurice's daughter? You could have brought me back some nice sporty type.

Some nice boy, pink from forest breezes, whom I could have moulded.

Moulded in what way?

Moulded in every way. Into whatever makes a good son-in-law.

But how can you mould a fifty-one-year-old, who's pushing seventy?

And inaudible.

Jean was wrong to tell me he he was inaudible.

That was the final blow.

Have a coffee in town, as if nothing's happened?

How can we pretend nothing's happened? Anyway, I never have coffee in town. The whole idea's a non-starter.

What should I do? Yet again, no idea.

The Captain of a Lost Ship.

The Woman There's always a photograph to look at.

A photograph to keep you company during the trip.

. . . In a tram in Prague in . . . 1964, there's a man sitting by the window. Looking out.

He has a high forehead, his eyes are sad, he's sixty –

He's holding his hand in front of his mouth in an attitude of contemplation which conceals half his face.

He's looking out.

Outside, there's a man standing on the pavement, with his hands in his pockets, watching the tram go by.

In the positions in which they find themselves, you could imagine that the two men were looking at each other. In fact, the two men are unaware of one another.

This encounter has no effect on either of them.

They don't even see each other.

What is it they're both looking at? The familiar course of time.

That's all they're looking at, time taking its familiar course.

If what happens happens purely by chance, there'd be no reason to dwell on this image.

There'd be no reason to dwell on anything.

My friend Serge is dead.

The world I'm looking at is a world in which my friend Serge no longer exists.

In his room at the hospital, in a drawer, there was a photograph of his mother.

A passport photo.

He took his mother with him for protection.

He was seventy-six. A man who'd been in positions of authority all his life, a grandfather himself, a man who you could say was more of a man than most, and he'd brought his mother with him, to keep in a drawer in his bedside table.

I ought to do it.

But I don't dare.

What's it matter anyhow?

And yet it does matter.

Suppose I summon up the courage to approach him between now and the time we arrive, well, I can't just sit here in silence and, without drawing attention to this coincidence in some way or another, start reading *The Unexpected Man*.

If I take *The Unexpected Man* out of my handbag, I'll have to lean towards him and say, excuse me, Mr Parsky, it just so happens I'm in the middle of reading *The Unexpected Man*, naturally I wouldn't be so insensitive as to read it in front of you –

He'll acknowledge me politely with a little smile.

And any conversation will be impossible, because that's the stupidest thing you could say.

The Man On the bridge the sailors run in all directions, some of them shouting the captain knows, others insisting the captain doesn't know. I go back to my cabin, the little Chinaman is there, pick up the rattle, I tell him, come on, little Chinaman, spin the rattle, assault my eardrums . . .

I shan't write any more.

The Captain will be my last.

Yuri must be in Buenos Aires by now.

Gone off with his Japanese on an Antarctic cruise. That's right.

It's the sort of trip you make when you've been round the world thirty-six times, you're in the twilight of your life, and what's left to you? Penguins.

Neurotics are the cream of humanity.

Inaudible.

No. No.

Mrs Cerda gets more and more cantankerous.

Jean says to me everyone else has a normal secretary and you have to have Mrs Cerda.

I have Mrs Cerda because, my boy, Mrs Cerda has been my secretary for twenty years. Which makes her absolutely irreplaceable. Yes, you have Mrs Cerda, who has her period thirty days in the month and doesn't even know how to switch on the computer.

Good! Good for her! It was stupid, buying that computer. We were fine. What did we need with a computer?

With the face and figure she's got, how could you be pleasant? She's bound to have complexes, poor woman.

All right, so she has complexes, she's not the first woman to be born ugly.

The curl of my lip is bitter.

Has it turned bitter because I'm bitter?

Or have I turned bitter through brooding on this physiological bitterness?

The feeling of getting old is bitter.

Yes. Shrivelling up is bitter.

I wasn't a bitter writer. No. No, I never wrote with bitterness.

I definitely shan't write any more.

The Captain of a Lost Ship will be my last.

The Captain of a Lost Ship, a clean book, straight up and down, the man I still hope to become.

The Woman My friend Serge didn't like your books.

It was our only quarrel.

He didn't like your short sentences, your repetitions.

He blamed you for your world view.

Negative, he used to say.

No, not at all negative.

I've never thought you were negative, Mr Parsky, quite the contrary.

All the same, what a coincidence, what a coincidence to find you sitting in front of me, in this compartment . . .

Serge, who didn't like your books and didn't like what he saw of you behind your books, said that your great stroke of luck was to have known how to make yourself lovable to me.

He said that whenever he read you, he was searching for that invisible quality which made me love you.

In the same way, I, not that I'd ever tell you this, I listened over and over again to that piece by Orlando Gibbons you're always talking about.

What attracted me towards you in the first place was your – I was going to say your love, but that's not the word, no, that's not the word at all – your nearness to music, your 'bond' with music, as if the key or the lack of key to everything was to be found there.

As if music was the thing in the world most lacking from the world.

And that's what you were searching for, since you wanted no truck with eternity as such.

My desires have always outstripped whatever actually happened.

Nothing ever lives up to desire. No.

And you see I can't understand why it is we're capable of desiring so much when in the end we feel so little.

Why is desire so extravagant compared to what actually happens?

You talked about this, Mr Parsky, in *A Passer-By Like Any Other,* where you're troubled about God and afraid that, just like the things you have experienced, God himself might not live up to your desire –

Let's come down to earth, dear, pretentious Mr Parsky, would you live up to my desire?

You with your highly polished shoes, your aristocratic fingernails, your mid-century elegance.

On the other hand, could I fetch out *The Unexpected Man* and not say a word?

Read without raising my eyes, occasionally looking out of the window, as if gripped by a fleeting thought . . .

I've spent my life with you, Mr Parsky.

That's to say, I've spent a few recent years of my life with you.

Which, all the same, means I've spent my life with you, because to arrive as close to you as I feel I have, I first had to reach the age I am and experience everything in the way I've experienced and understood it.

To be able to follow you down your road to what looks like excess, I've had to practise all my life.

This is what I think.

You manufacture yourself, you shape the raw material, then you lay it open to the unexpected.

For a long time I've been attracted by people who don't care for the world and are tormented by non-stop suffering.

It seemed to me that the desperate were the only profound, the only really attractive people.

Fundamentally, if I'm honest, I thought them superior.

For a long time I felt myself to be less interesting, not to say less admirable, because I loved life.

Whereas you, you claim not to love anything, you complain about everything, but in your rage, in your vitriolic energy, I see life itself.

And, not wishing to infuriate you, I also see joy.

I talk to you secretly. Secretly, I tell you everything I can never tell you.

How to approach you, you in the twilight of your life, I in mine, and say something appropriate to our age?

Read without saying a word.

Are you even going to notice?

Have you even looked my way?

Since our journey began, have you raised your eyes in my direction one single time?

When I'm not facing towards you, I feel as if you're watching me, but when I decide to connect with you silently, you're somewhere else.

The Man Detested the way Elie spoke to me about *The Unexpected Man*.

Detested it so much, I can't bear to see him again.

I'm repeating myself. So?

I'm repeating myself. Yes. Well, of course, I'm repeating myself.

That's what I do. What else is there to do?

In fact, little Elie, you didn't even use the phrase 'repeat yourself'. If you'd said, 'You're repeating yourself,' I would have sensed some small degree of pleasant

85

familiarity in the 'You're repeating yourself,' I would have discerned the affection, the affectionate bluntness of a friend. What you did say, so embarrassed you were squirming around like a woman, was it's very like, it's very like things you've written before. Things I've written before which you adored, Elie Breitling!

Except now, there's been a change of idol.

What you adored, you adored when it was new, 'undissected', on the fringes of fashion.

Not original, but new.

I emphasise new, and not original. Two diametrically opposed concepts.

When it comes to it, you've never had the patience, the discreet patience for unconditional love.

The craze for novelty.

Is it what are you actually saying? No. It's what are you saying that's new?

What's new?

Who's your new idol, little Elie?

Of course, I could always find out by reading your column . . . it's ages since I gave up reading your column.

Did I ever read it? Even when you were the pioneer of my ultra-novelty, acclaiming in your articles all my worst qualities.

Bitter.

Could I possibly have turned bitter?

No.

The Woman You're a man with whom I'd like to have discussed certain things.

In fact, people with whom you'd like to discuss things are not all that thick on the ground.

I, who was so biased in favour of men, finished up by turning my back on their friendships.

My best friends, my few rare and singular friends, are women.

That women would turn out to be better friends to me than men is a development I could never have predicted.

Apart from my friend Serge, who's now dead, I had another friend.

His name was Georges.

Georges was slightly in love with me.

In that charming way men have of being slightly in love with you, without expecting anything. I was married.

And our friendship contained a hint of mischief, a . . . how shall I put it, a knowing closeness.

I laughed a great deal with Georges, Mr Parsky. You know how it is when you can laugh. By the way, I've often laughed in your company.

One day, Georges arrived with a woman.

He thought it acceptable to introduce a woman into our relationship. He committed the solecism of comparing us.

I am not a woman, Mr Parsky, who invites comparisons.

Nor am I a woman to be weighed against anyone or anything.

Sixteen years of friendship and he still hadn't grasped that.

Worse, he confided in me.

Worse still, he asked my advice.

Sixteen years of pleasantly double-edged friendship collapsed in three sentences.

The poor man didn't even realise – of course, when I say the poor man I'm speaking purely from my point of view – because he was, and this was what was most intolerable: happy.

Happy, Mr Parsky.

I was very civilised about it.

To have so often been civilised about things is perhaps where I've gone wrong in life.

Georges married this woman – she was one of his patients, Georges is a dentist – and he had a child.

We used to have lunch occasionally.

We both went on pretending we were still intimates.

To start with, Georges kept his end up.

Our conversations, although meatless, because the meat of a conversation obviously doesn't lie in what's actually said, still retained the glow of our old conversations.

And then, feeling free, God knows why, as time went on, Georges began to talk to me about his son.

A certain Eric.

How Georges could have called his son Eric remains a mystery to me.

We never talked about my children – I have two – although he no doubt remembered I was a mother myself.

Among parents you expect a bit of mutual unbosoming, don't you?

Eric was a treasure, Mr Parsky. A little treasure.

You put him to bed. Bam, he was asleep.

You woke him up. He started gurgling.

His little hands were so strong. His little arms were so loving. Eric sang all day long. The father was happy, the child was secure, what could be more natural?

One day, Georges said to me quite seriously, with tears in his eyes, when I take him out in his pushchair, I'm sorry for the people who walk past without smiling at him.

Out of Georges's mouth, the word 'pushchair'!

The least domesticated of men. Or so I thought.

A man I'd known as outrageous and insolent, reduced to shreds, liquefied by paternity.

And who, with no memory of himself or me, sat there boasting of his liquefaction.

One evening, and I'm finally getting to what I wanted to tell you in the first place, we went to listen to some

Brahms sonatas. It was a long time since we'd spent an evening together.

After the concert, he took me to a Thai restaurant I particularly liked and after dinner we had a drink at the Crillon bar.

How can I explain this to you? The whole evening had gone by under some star unshackled from time. Not a word about Eric, or pushchairs, not a word about married patients, just a couple of could-be lovers, as in the past, arm-in-arm, laughing, faintly disreputable.

He took me back to my house. He walked me.

He walked me because he didn't have his car.

As we walked, I felt able to flirt quite freely as before and the air was sweet.

In front of my door, where, in earlier days, we would linger, sometimes for hours, I suddenly had the feeling he was in a hurry . . .

We said goodnight with an impersonal kiss and I watched him running, Mr Parsky, running, racing to look for a taxi, running desperately back to his little family, back to his own, running like a man who'd finally snapped his chains –

The Man I don't see why I shouldn't go back on Ex-Lax.

I was happy with Ex-Lax.

Jean says it's dangerous. What is he, a doctor? When all's said and done, I don't see why I should listen to my son, who isn't a doctor and who, not content with being round-shouldered, smokes.

Ex-Lax suited me.

It was a comfortable way to download.

Curious word, 'download'. We never said download in my day.

Ex-Lax was a success.

Full stop.

Can never remember the name of that quasi-son-in-law.

Henri? Gérard? – Rémy?

Rémy Sledz.

Sledz. Yes.

'Mr Sledz, you're planning to live with my daughter –'
Don't be stupid, they've been living together for months.

'Mr Sledz, you're planning to –' Ugh, I refuse to utter
the verb 'marry', the verb 'marry' is not in my repertoire.

'Mr Sledz, I imagine you must appreciate a father's
concerns –' If he answers, of course, I keep putting myself
in your shoes, I'll strangle him with my bare hands.

Stay cool. Don't get involved.

Is it right for me to get involved in her life?

What is it that counts? The long run? Or the moment?
What is it that's really of value?

In the train carrying him from Paris to Frankfurt, Paul
Parsky still has no idea of the value of time.

I refuse to give in.

No surrender.

The Woman You once said in an interview that as a
writer you had no opinions and that you had no
intention of saying anything whatsoever on any given
subject, and that you greatly admired philosophers, or
great mathematicians, anyone from the world of ideas,
and that you yourself had done nothing but notice
certain things and interpret what you'd noticed, but that
never, never in a million years, had your writing shown
any tendency or inclination to enter the world of ideas.

You said in this interview that ideas about the world
were strictly speaking of no value in the practice of
literature.

Sheer hypocrisy.

I've never found anything in any of your books which
doesn't express in a completely personal way your view
of the world.

Even your energy is a view of the world.

Your allergy to nuance is a view of the world.

Your disinclination to do the sensible thing is a view of the world.

Reading your interview, I finally grasped something unexpected: your fear of being understood, Mr Parsky.

You cover your tracks, you personally invent protective misunderstandings, because you're haunted by the fear of being understood.

Pursued, yes.

Understood, no.

A judicious helping of impenetrability is how you avert this great misfortune and preserve your prestige intact.

In *The Unexpected Man*, which is in my handbag, your hero, your alter ego, claims he only wanted to be someone in order to be able to abdicate.

When are you, my dear writer, planning to abdicate?

I see no signs of abdication anywhere.

Not in your flirtatious isolation, and not in those immoderately offhand comments you squeeze out about yourself.

And certainly not in your writing.

In *The Unexpected Man*, which I have in my handbag, you don't for one second give up any of the illusions of the human race.

If ever a man was far from giving them up, it's you, my poor old thing.

Absurd to feel intimidated by you.

Really ridiculous.

'Mr Parsky, chance, wonderful chance – or rather, chance, quite simply – chance has decreed that I should meet you on this train; I can't resist telling you . . .'

And what are you going to tell him?

How will you fight your way back up from that kind of affectation?

'Mr Parsky, I'm prepared to risk any kind of adventure with you.'

Just to see his face.

If he laughs, if he genuinely laughs, he's the man I think he is.

Come on, Martha, life is short.

And what if he doesn't laugh?

If he doesn't laugh, he's not the man you think he is, so you'll wind down the window and throw out *The Unexpected Man*.

And you'll be so ashamed, you'll throw yourself out after it.

And what if he genuinely does laugh?

If he genuinely does laugh . . .

This is torture! . . .

The Man Can never sleep on a train.

Hard enough in bed, let alone on a train.

Strange this woman never reads anything.

A woman who doesn't read anything the whole journey.

Not even a spot of *Marie Claire*.

Perhaps I should write for the theatre?

No, no, no . . . God, no!

How could it even cross my mind!

Something must have come loose in my brain.

Besides, in the theatre, the only thing I can stand is boulevard comedy.

Basically.

At a boulevard comedy, the audience laughs like normal people.

They don't laugh in that deathly way you hear these days in the palaces of culture.

Laughter congratulating itself for being intelligent enough to know why it's being laughed.

A little *in* laugh in several stages.

The way Elie Breitling laughed during *Measure for Measure*.

That's right. That's the way Elie laughs these days.

It's something new. He never used to laugh like that.
No, no, there was a time, when Elie was in a crowd, he laughed like a normal person.

A time when Elie would have talked to me about *The Unexpected Man* in his kitchen at three o'clock in the morning in front of his fifteenth Fernet Branca and I would have hung on every word.

Is there today one single person in the whole world, in the whole world, who might know how to read that book?

The Woman I'm not on good terms with Nadine, Serge's wife.

Serge used to have adventures, and she knew I knew.
She thought I condoned them.
It's a pity our relationship disintegrated.
Nadine always respected my friendship with Serge.
She's an intelligent woman.
Things deteriorated when Serge started to have adventures.

Adventures – may be something of an exaggeration. Anyway.

As she got older, Nadine blew up like a balloon. And when a woman blows up like a balloon, a man begins to look elsewhere.

I'm talking to you about Serge, Mr Parsky, because Serge was one of your characters.

He didn't like you, but if they were to read you, would your characters like you?

Let's imagine Strattmer reading *The Unexpected Man*.
I'd say he'd get impatient after about two pages.
Like Strattmer, Serge was an insomniac.

One night, when he couldn't sleep and he was tossing and turning in his bed, he tried to calm himself by thinking about Auschwitz.

He conjured up the discomfort of the mattresses, the stench of the latrines, the lack of space. Here you are, he said to himself, in your soft bed with your clean sheets, you don't have some neighbour's stinking feet in your mouth, you don't have to get up and carry away that disgusting bucket: so go to sleep!

Go to sleep, Serge old chap!

Just at the moment he was about to fall asleep, he said to himself, wait a minute! An idea which ought to haunt you, and give you no peace, and you're using it as a soporific!

A horror which you did not experience, and you're turning it into a tranquilliser?!

He wanted to write something about this confusion. He got up to look for some paper.

Couldn't find any.

I woke Nadine up, he told me, she, let's be fair, has no need to think about Auschwitz to get off to sleep, and I said how can it be possible, how can it be possible I said, this is what Serge told me, and you can see how calm I am, I'm saying this very calmly, how can it be possible that there is not one piece of paper in this house?

I can't bear people who sleep.

How can people sleep? How can they sleep well?

If I may say so, Martha – Serge was seventeen years older than me and we always maintained a certain formality – if I may say so, Martha, I know you're a poor sleeper and that is the cornerstone of our friendship. Nadine sleeps. It's her latest enthusiasm. She's a sleeper.

She used to be a woman you could rely on for a conversation any time of the night.

One day, I shall publish my theory about sleepers.

We were having lunch that day – as a hypochondriac, Serge left you standing – and I said to him, you're looking bonny. What do you mean, I'm looking bonny! I haven't slept a wink all night and I'm looking bonny?! Perhaps it's a circulation problem?!

He got up and went to check his complexion in the gents!

Before he died, he said to me, I don't want a single word spoken at my funeral.

Be so good as to be there to check.

As for music, I'd be happy with Schumann, but I wouldn't want to seem too romantic.

Be honest, Mr Parsky, Serge is one of your characters, isn't he?

Mr Parsky, I'm afraid I miss my friend Serge terribly.

The Man To think, all those years, and I knew nothing about Debussy.

Thirty years without hearing a note of Debussy.

I got through 'Clair de Lune' all right the day before yesterday.

For the teacher to suggest 'La Cathédrale engloutie', he must have been impressed by the progress I've made.

Good idea to take up the piano again.

There's been a maturing . . . a mental leap forward . . .

How could Nathalie have said to me that Yuri plays better than I do?

Has she no ear?

Well, of course it's true I don't attempt the same pieces as Mr Yuri Kogloff. I don't attempt Scriabin, I don't play 'L'Ile joyeuse'.

I'm too fond of music.

He even plays 'Scarbo'.

It's all wrong, the tempo's shot to hell, bum notes from beginning to end.

He plays like an old Jewish refugee in a bar.

And my own daughter is taken in.

She tells me I don't know how to use the pedal.

She's right.

In any case, I use it less and less.

Pieces which require the pedal are few and far between.

Even Schubert. Even with Schubert, I manage that 'Impromptu' very well without bothering with the pedal.

I play it very efficiently. All right, in an ideal world, you'd use the pedal, if you knew how to. But without the pedal, it's not bad at all, in fact it's rather good.

Yuri knows all about the pedal.

When Yuri sits down at the piano, his Japanese is ecstatic.

Yuri will play in front of anyone.

He has no shame.

The more he waters it down, the better his Japanese likes it.

It's true I'm ready to attempt 'La Cathédrale engloutie'.

There are two reasons behind my progress.

First, I'm getting better and better at sight-reading. Thanks to Bach, I've got used to a strong, quick left hand, which compels you to anticipate.

And secondly, I've succeeded in hearing myself.

Easy enough to hear other people play. It's hearing oneself, that's what's difficult.

I have to ask my teacher to let me work on some of the 'Waldszenen'.

I've always had a feeling for Schumann. Now that I've matured.

'Vogel als Prophet', that's what I must play. That'll be my next piece.

If I were a painter, I'd draw this woman's face.

It's a disturbing face. Cold . . . no, disturbingly indifferent.

A woman who might fire the imagination.

The Woman When Serge said to me before he died that he wanted Schumann at his funeral, but that he was afraid of seeming too romantic, I laughed.

Of course I laughed. But he said, how can you laugh?

Don't you remember when you had your hip operation and were convinced you'd never come round from the anaesthetic, you said to me, if I die, whatever you do don't let them put my age in *Le Figaro*!

Which of us is the more frivolous?

Frivolous beyond the grave, we are.

How to accept that somebody we loved is dead.

How to accept that the world contains one less person to love us . . .

My parents are gone.

A husband I loved, gone.

So many friends, dead.

Serge, dead.

How to accept never being in control of time or loneliness.

It was a good idea to have my hair done before I left.

Last time she made it too blonde, but this time she's done it well.

And I was right to wear my yellow suit. I needn't have worried I'd be cold in it and it gives me an air of mystery.

If that idiotic writer deigned to glance over in my direction, he would see me at my best.

At least that's some satisfaction.

Do you really think man hasn't changed since the stone age?

I'm dying to ask you the question. Do you really think, as you maintain the whole way through *The Unexpected Man*, that man's knowledge is the only thing about him that's evolved?

It's not your invention, the theory that knowledge makes no difference.

Of course it isn't, but you develop it with such bitterness.

Your outlook is so bitter.

If I insist on talking to you – even though it's in secret – about Serge, it's because in my mind there are so many ways the two of you are connected.

One day I called him, stupidly excited about the fall of the Berlin Wall. Fine, he said, yes, so what? Its coming down won't improve the behaviour of mankind.

Deep down I wonder if there wasn't a touch of jealousy in his antipathy towards you; it must have annoyed him that I kept unearthing his character and his thoughts in your books. Another time we were talking about Tiananmen Square and he said I couldn't care less about the Chinese students, I still prefer the Iranians.

I prefer whirling dervishes to human rights.

Serge, always excessive, like Strattmer, and like you.

Not an ounce of self-restraint.

An attractiveness essentially based on character flaws.

I was so low when I packed last night!

Do men ever suffer that kind of low?

Still felt sad this morning.

Sad at the station.

A woman who travels from Paris to Frankfurt with nothing else to read but *The Unexpected Man* is a deeply depressed woman.

One day I'd like someone to explain to me why sadness always catches you by surprise, when everything seems under control.

What the hell, I'm fetching out the book.

I'm fetching out the book. I'll place myself so he can see me. He can't not react. He can't watch me embarking on an intimate relationship with him six feet away without revealing himself. What are you going to do in Frankfurt?

The Book Fair? No. First of all, I don't think it's the time of year, and a writer with your nature, flirtatiously antisocial, doesn't turn up at the Book Fair.

So what can you be doing there?

Oh, God, make him speak to me.

The Man What's she going to do in Frankfurt?
   Visit a relative? Work?
   No, she has a lover in the petrochemical industry.
   This woman doesn't have a husband, she has a lover.
In the petrochemical industry. Excellent.
   Unless she's quite simply German.
   On her way home.
   She's not German. No.
   Why? Why isn't she German?
   At any rate, if she's German, she's not from Frankfurt.
Anyway, no, she isn't a German. Germans don't look out
of the window like that. She's a woman who's going
somewhere. Not a woman who's coming back.
   Should I approach her?
   What would I say?
   What's it matter if she's German or what she is? But, ·
yes, the worm is in the bud, I have to know.
   I'll approach her.

He speaks to her.

Please excuse me, do you think we might open the
window a bit?

The Woman Yes, it is quite warm. By all means.

You answered my prayer!
   Such a trivial prayer and you answered it!
   Listened to a couple of insignificant words which
could have no possible bearing on the higher course of
time and tide.
   Oh, God, have I ever once prayed to you without
asking for a favour?
   Maybe I ought not to get to know you, Mr Parsky.
   Suppose I don't like you, why take the risk of no
longer being able to love anything about you?

I'm told there isn't necessarily an intimate link between a man and his work.

How can that be possible?

I should have . . . I should have said something else instead of smiling like a fool. I was caught on the hop.

Now he's sunk back, deep in his thoughts.

What a dimwit.

After all, I have a perfect right to break the silence as well.

Even if I only do it once.

But what would I say?

Something absolutely banal would be most appropriate, least heavy.

Whatever else happens, I don't want to make him think I'm jumping feet first into a conversation.

What leads on from the window? . . .

The Man French. I knew it.

French. An affecting voice.

A hint of strangeness.

Her lover's a conductor. Why not?

He's about to conduct 'Verklärte Nacht'.

Afterwards you'll spend the night in Wiesbaden.

Friday you'll be in Mainz, where you'll buy a painting which strongly resembles you, by some minor *cinquecento* master.

The painting is called *The Portrait and Dream of Giovanna Alviste*.

In it you're leaning forward slightly, three-quarters in shadow, looking out of a window at a blurred landscape with a bridge.

Both of you stopped dead in front of the painting in the antique shop. Because there on the canvas, melancholy in the moonlight, are your unmistakable features, your very particular eyes, gazing out in a distinctively watchful and supercilious way.

You buy the painting. No, not you, the conductor buys the painting.

He tells you he's going to keep it in his bedroom so he can contemplate you every day with complete impunity.

You laugh.

You laugh and try to remember who you were when you were *Giovanna Alviste*.

A splinter of life among so many others, a tiny pinprick in time, amid so much pointless loneliness, so many heaped-up splinters, scraps of dead wood scattered across our paths . . .

Bitter.

Why did I pay for Mrs Cerda to go to Biarritz?

What could have prompted such generosity?

Her great bollocks of a son was there. She was hoping to avert some cock-up by offering him a scooter.

I've always regretted my moments of virtue.

All those 'noble' gestures, after the event I've always discovered some tainted reason for having made them.

Mrs Cerda's been a complete wreck since the collapse of Communism.

The only life Mrs Cerda knew was standing firm against the Reds.

In a case like that, what's the use of Biarritz?

Nathalie told me that . . . what's his name again . . .?

Sledz. Sledz adored *A Passer-By Like Any Other*.

People keep talking to me about books I wrote thirty years ago!

I can't even remember what it was about. Seriously, I've no idea.

He liked *A Passer-By Like Any Other*, so did everybody else, great, obviously he read it a couple of weeks ago, as far as he's concerned it's the present, Paul Parsky in the present, whereas for me it's a book written by somebody quite other.

There's some misunderstanding about time.

What we produce stagnates. Ossifies. Only plays an active part in other people's minds.

In time what a man produces becomes what's furthest from him.

To start with, what's he doing reading *A Passer-By Like Any Other*? Instead of, let's say, *The Remark*, which is far better. Not to mention *The Unexpected Man*.

Which actually I would have disapproved of, because it's too recent.

All in all, I prefer it that he's dug up the *Passer-By*, rather than plunging into *The Unexpected Man*.

Plunging into *The Unexpected Man* before he'd met me would have been the worst, the worst sort of blunder.

. . . 'Mr Sledz, my trip to Frankfurt has given me a chance to reassess our situation . . .'

What do you mean, *our*? He couldn't care less about *my* situation.

That's exactly what I have against him! He has no consideration for me!

The Woman I like travelling.

As soon as I set foot in Frankfurt, I shall be another person: the one who arrives is always another person.

And so it is that one progresses, from one person to another, until it's all over.

Mr Parsky, you rested your eyes on me in a certain way, there was a question mark in your bright eyes.

For a brief instant in your life, possibly imperceptible even to yourself, I'm sure I had some effect on you.

What was your question?

Whatever it is, the answer's yes.

Yes, it's me.

I'm the one who, secretly, one day, will make off with your world, I'm the one, I'll make off with your light, your face, your happy hours or sad, the days and nights your name is on, the whole of time to ashes.

I'm the one. The one who loved you, who coloured you according to my inclinations, the one who studied every subject under your perpetual catechism, I shall abolish you, I shall make off with you when my time is up and nothing will remain of you or of anything else.

That was my answer when you rested your eyes on me and spoke to me of fresh air.

I have a brother, who lives in Paris. Older than me.

We keep on talking about other people, because we're made up of other people, don't you agree?

As a writer, you know that better than anyone.

My brother lives in Paris, in a handsome apartment building in the 17th *arrondissement*.

The hallway in his building is paved with white, beige and black flagstones.

He's been living in his building for twenty-five years, and for twenty-five years, every day that God sends, my brother has only stepped on the light-coloured flagstones, alternating, according to a very precise and never varying formula, between white and beige.

Never, in twenty-five years, has he stepped on a black flagstone.

And anybody with him is forbidden to step on the black flagstones, which are somehow more tempting than the others.

When he inadvertently passes the concierge, on whom he's never dared impose his ban, he closes his eyes so as not to witness her sacrilege.

He told me he was petitioning the Residents' Association to have her replaced because, and I quote, she was an irresponsible woman who, in defiance of all common sense, was pulverising the chessboard.

My brother is convinced that the world order depends on the flawlessness of his passage.

A world order which comprises all possible journeys, including, Mr Parsky, ours in this Paris to Frankfurt train.

And if, in turn, I make so bold as to address you, it will be because, in the great labyrinth of life, my brother or I, according to the rules, have happened to stand on the correct stone.

Right. That's enough philosophising.

We're already beyond Strasbourg. Time for action.

Some banal phrase. No.

I'm fetching out the book.

She fetches The Unexpected Man *out of her handbag.*

The funniest thing would be if he didn't even notice.

Come on, Martha, employ a little cunning in the way you read.

Discreet but unmistakably strong on presence.

My heart is beating.

I'm twelve years old – what a trip!

The Man How many times in my youth did I think, ah, old age! – happiness – calm – no more pretence!

Buffoon!

Ah, old age! Now what's it look like?

An old boy with a rancorous expression. The kind of man who takes umbrage when his old friend Breitling utters the ghost of a reservation.

No, no. No, it wasn't the ghost of a reservation.

Let's not understate it.

And if we didn't care what people said to us, why would we struggle on with a pursuit which is at the mercy of outside opinion?

An old man in thrall to the judgements of his contemporaries, condemned, whatever he may say, to try to put a good face on it.

But for whose benefit? For whose benefit?

She's reading.

She's reading *The Unexpected Man!* . . .

Extraordinary . . .

Where's she got to?

Page . . . page . . . 120? . . .

Extraordinary . . .

120 . . . Strattmer's in hospital.

He's already met Reuvens. She must have read the chapter about the counting mania. Or else she's in the middle of it.

No, she's not laughing, she must have finished reading it. Unless she's in the middle of it and she doesn't think it's funny. No, no.

This woman would be laughing. I'm sure of it. She must have gone past it.

You couldn't read about the counting mania without at least smiling.

She is smiling! She's smiling! She's in the middle of it!

Strattmer meets Reuvens who talks to him about his counting mania, which Strattmer also suffers from – one of many.

Don't stare at her so insistently. You'll break her concentration.

Extraordinary –

She doesn't know who I am, no. No, of course not.

She wouldn't just be innocently reading like that. She doesn't know who I am.

Why didn't she start reading it when we set off?

Lack of interest. No. Just look at her expression.

A good face on it for whose benefit? For whose benefit, my old Parsky? Why, for hers, for your unforeseen travelling companion, this silent woman sent to you by fate, the focus of your beseeching gaze.

She's reading *The Unexpected Man*.

It's really too much.

I knew she was an interesting woman.

Shall I remain anonymous?

Why wasn't she reading it when we set off?

Because she had things to think about.

In Frankfurt, she's going to break up with the conductor.
She was thinking about methods of breaking up.

About turns of phrase to use when breaking up. In their relationship they've always weighed their words.

She's going to break up with the conductor and *The Unexpected Man is* the book she's chosen as witness to this moment.

Remain anonymous? Absolutely.

But aren't I likely to feel some sort of bitterness?

As usual. What's the point of these scruples?

Which will probably deprive me of a simple pleasure.

Anyway, it's not so much scruples, as you hasten to flatter yourself, it's more like discretion, not to say cowardice.

Isn't the benefit I might derive from this strange occurrence, by simply remembering it and passing it on to others, enough?

Not enough.

I have to reveal myself.

But maybe in two stages.

The Woman '. . . As far as my daughter's concerned, Strattmer, I consider myself unclean. I've always been afraid of infecting her. I was tidying away some fish scraps in the kitchen, when I spotted a slice of lime. I licked it; I like the taste, it reminds me of Mexico. I put it back on the table. I said to myself, you can't leave it there, contaminated, where anyone could pick it up. You can't throw it away, it cost you one franc seventy-five, it's a lime, they're hard to come by. So I bit into it and chewed it until it was ready to be thrown away. During these five minutes of oral acidity, I performed the electrified dance imposed on me by my limbs and took the opportunity to tot up the number of cupboard handles in the room, items which curiously enough I had never previously counted.'

How strange that I was telling you about my brother.

This counting mania is exactly what my brother suffers from.

My brother is the victim of counting mania and, to that extent, he's also part of your universe.

Oh, my God, what you write about is so familiar to me!

And you're so far away.

I've made a mistake.

You're not going to speak to me.

There was a time, Mr Parsky, when I had no need to get embroiled in books and handbags and failures of nerve . . .

I was beautiful and that spoke for me.

He's seen me.

He's watching me, he's seen the book.

Here we go.

I didn't wear my yellow suit for nothing.

I didn't get into this compartment for nothing.

Nothing's for nothing.

I'll count to twenty and then I'll say . . .

What will you say, Martha?

I'll say . . .

Think of the sentence and then count.

The Man A famous author goes on a journey and sits opposite an unknown woman who's reading his latest book.

Good subject for a short story.

Bit old-fashioned.

Could have been written by . . . by whom?

Stefan Zweig. Yes . . . Or Manuel Torga – Yes.

The man's intimidated.

A man who prides himself on having outgrown such childishness is suddenly touched by the indelicacy of the situation.

The woman's attractive.

Would he be intimidated if the woman wasn't attractive?

If the woman wasn't attractive, he would withdraw into his distaste for what's called the public, that breed never to be encountered.

Let's be honest. You've never done anything for no reason or for nobody. You don't create in a void.

You throw bottles into the sea desperately hoping for a castaway.

To produce, to add to the world is to experience the magic of possibility. Here goes.

How would you account for the need to invent or dream up other lives?

Isn't it enough quite simply to exist, what do you think?

The Woman I don't know what you mean by quite simply to exist. There's no such thing as quite simply.

The Man That book you're holding, it so happens I've read it as well –

The Woman Oh, really? . . .

The Man Do you like it?

The Woman I'm not sure I can answer such a blunt question. This is an author I've been close to for some time . . .

The Man You as well.

The Woman You as well?

The Man For some time. Yes. What have you read?

The Woman *A Passer-By Like Any Other . . . A* small collection of short stories, can't remember the title . . . *The Remark, The Poor Man's Footstep . . .*

The Man Did you like *The Poor Man's Footstep*?

The Woman Yes . . . For me, it's the most moving. What about you?

The Man . . . I remember it as being quite a personal book.

The Woman Yes, that's what I'd say. Personal. Inevitable. And which must have felt inevitable to the man who wrote it.

The Man Could be. You can't always write like that.

The Woman No. I'm sure.

The Man You can only lay yourself naked once.

The Woman I'm sure.

Pause.

The Man You don't want to talk to me about this book?

The Woman I can't talk about it before I've finished it.

The Man Yes, you can. I mean, the ending has no significance.

The Woman Well . . . the book says the same thing to me as that photograph of Prague above your head . . . It's given me, yet again, a nostalgia for what's never taken place.
A nostalgia for what might happen.
Does it deal with anything else?

The Man Don't you find it irritatingly repetitious?

The Woman Yes. But I never read without being irritated. He's a deeply irritating writer.

The Man He certainly is.

The Woman You find him irritating as well?

The Man Yes, yes, irritating. Very irritating. Are you going to Frankfurt?

The Woman Yes.

Pause.

The Man He's an irritating writer and in my view a minor writer.
You're quite wrong to interest yourself in him.

The Woman Irritating, yes. Minor, no.
Everything you love is irritating.

The Man He's a selfish little busybody who's never been able to turn a single moment into an eternity, which is the mark of a poet, he can't speak of death except cynically, sniggering like some pathetic old hag, he claims to hate the crowd and the masses, but he's never known how to describe man's unhappiness, the only sadness he can talk about is his own, about which he is maniacally repetitious! There's a sentence he envies in an elegy by Borges: 'On the other side of the door,' Borges says, 'a man made out of love, of time and of loneliness has just been weeping in Buenos Aires for everything that is.' You see, Paul Parsky has never known how to weep for everything that is.

Silence.

The Woman I think you're very unfair.
But I don't believe you mean it, since you said all that with the kind of effrontery which implies the opposite.
In *The Remark,* he sees a middle-aged woman in a Metro station, a fat woman with a shawl and a heavy coat. She's crying, her face is pressed up against the grubby white tiles of the wall, right next to a poster for *Holiday on Ice.*

She has slippers on her feet, and ankle-socks pulled up over her swollen calves.

He describes her feet, her slippers, the bruised skin between her socks and her coat and through this the whole of her life, her entire life in five lines . . .

In another book, he talks about watching his grandfather out of the window as he turns the corner by the house and tiptoes away like a child, clutching the results of his medical tests.

And in *The Unexpected Man*, come to that, there's that woman who has lunch by herself every Sunday at the Blue Sea Hotel in Royan, plastered with make-up, her hair dyed, dressed in pink, ridiculed and sneered at by everybody, about whom nevertheless you say . . . that she was kindness itself . . . All these things and so many others you've described, Mr Parsky, have made me weep . . .

You have no right to be bitter. In your books there have been hundreds of moments like eternity. And if I have to prove myself worthy of whatever devil has dropped me down in this compartment, I'm forced to admit I've been madly in love with you and that in another life – since I wouldn't like to embarrass you – I would have taken off with you, on any kind of adventure . . .

He laughs.

CONVERSATIONS AFTER A BURIAL

Conversations After a Burial was first performed at
the Almeida Theatre, London, on 7 September 2000.
The cast was as follows:

Nathan Matthew Marsh
Édith Amanda Root
Alex Paul Higgins
Pierre David Calder
Julienne Claire Bloom
Élisa Clare Holman

Director Howard Davies
Designer Rob Howell
Lighting Mark Henderson
Music Dominic Muldowney
Sound John A. Leonard and Fergus O'Hare

Characters

Nathan
forty-eight

Édith
forty-five

Alex
forty-three, Nathan and Édith's brother

Pierre
sixty-five, their uncle, their mother's brother

Julienne
sixty-four, his wife

Élisa
thirty-five, Alex's ex-mistress

Setting

The family property in the Loiret.

Nothing realistic.

A single open space.

The woods, the clearing and the house
are simply suggested, with different elements,
so that blackouts, whether during or between
scenes, can be as brief as possible.

One

Noon.
In the silence of the undergrowth, a man is covering his father's coffin with earth. Then he moves away.
Nathan, Édith and Alex stand, motionless. Pierre and Julienne are further off. Somewhat in the background is Élisa. Nathan takes a piece of paper out of his pocket and reads aloud.

Nathan 'When my mother died, I was six. She was walking upstairs with her suitcase and I can remember the suitcase skidding across the flagstones. When my father passed away, I was eleven and it was war time . . . I found myself alone in the world, so alone and so instantly awake that I was visited by the Devil . . . I welcomed him as a strategic reinforcement, a rampart on my fortress where I could slip away, sheltered from the loopholes. From that day and ever afterwards, I confronted life, bristling with spines from head to toe, stainless and icy. I gave my imaginary son the name of Nathan. For your sake, Nathan, my dazzling spark, may Heaven grant I do not die too soon. Simon Weinberg, 1928.' Dad was twenty.

Blackout.

Two

A terrace. On a level with the house. A table. Some garden chairs. Alex and Nathan, standing.

Nathan Where have you been?

Alex My room.

Nathan I called you, you didn't answer.

Alex Has she gone?

Nathan I don't know.

Alex Who told her?

Nathan I don't know . . .

Alex You did.

Nathan No.

Édith appears.

Édith It was me . . . I told her.

Alex You told her to come?

Édith No. (*Pause.*) What's it matter?

Alex Has she gone?

Édith No.

Alex Tell her to bugger off.

Édith Stop it . . .

Alex Tell her to bugger off. Please.

Silence.

Édith Would you like me to make some coffee?

Alex There's something obscene about it!

Édith Listen, Alex, this isn't quite the moment, don't you think . . .

Nathan Leave him alone.

Édith They saw each other, you know, she even came here without telling you.

Alex So?

Édith I mean, there's nothing abnormal about her being here . . .

Alex I suppose if you go and visit someone, you feel you have to go to their funeral! You poor thing, you must spend your life at funerals!

Nathan Will you make some coffee, Édith?

Édith Yes . . .

Alex Leave it. I'll do it. (*As he goes.*) No doubt I'm the one who's abnormal.

Nathan It's your behaviour that's abnormal.

Alex looks at Nathan, then leaves. Édith sits down. Silence.
    Élisa appears.

Édith Sit down . . . Come and sit down . . .

Élisa No, I won't stay, thank you . . . I just came to say goodbye . . . Goodbye, Édith . . .

They embrace.

. . . Goodbye, Nathan . . . (*She moves towards him and hesitates, then holds out her hand. She half turns.*)

Nathan Élisa . . .

Élisa Yes?

Nathan Stay a while . . .

Édith Alex has gone to make some coffee, stay a little while . . .

Élisa He'll be back . . .

Pause.

Nathan Where's my uncle?

Élisa He's gone down the road for a walk, with his wife.

Nathan Do you know her?

Élisa No.

Nathan Sit down.

Élisa No . . .

Nathan If I sit down, will you sit down?

Élisa No . . .

Alex (*voice-over*) Édith, where are the filter-papers?

Édith Above the sink . . . (*She gets up and leaves.*)

Silence.

Nathan You've cut your hair.

Élisa Yes . . . quite a long time ago.

Nathan It's nice . . .

Élisa You think so?

Nathan Yes.

Élisa I have to go . . .

Silence.

Nathan Goodbye.

Élisa Goodbye. (*She half turns, then moves back towards him. Very quickly*) Nathan, I don't suppose we'll ever see each other again, there's something I have to say to you . . . For years now, I've only had one thing in my mind, to see you again, I've only had one obsession, to see you again, to see you, to hear your voice . . . My life's been haunted by you, I'm incapable of loving anybody else . . .

> *She turns away and leaves very quickly. Nathan remains, on his own.*
> *Darkness.*

> *Same scene, same lighting. Nathan is alone. Édith appears, carrying coffee cups.*

Édith Has she gone?

Nathan Yes.

> *Edith puts the cups on the table.*

Édith Jean just phoned. I almost invited him to lunch tomorrow and then I thought . . . Actually I don't much want to see him, well, not him exactly, but . . . He's been posted to London.

Nathan Is he pleased?

Édith I imagine so. (*She smiles.*) Although he announced it to me in his sinister voice . . .

> *Nathan smiles.*

Aren't you hot? I don't know why I'm so hot . . . (*She takes off her cardigan.*) You'd think it was September . . . She was right to leave.

123

Alex appears with the coffee pot.

Alex It'll be weak, I had to scrape the bottom of the packet.

Nathan In the cupboard in the pantry?

Alex Didn't look in there.

Édith It's the first time I've seen you make coffee.

Alex How do you imagine I survive?

Édith I didn't say you didn't know how to. You take everything the wrong way.

Alex I don't take everything the wrong way, now what have I said? It's just you seem to think it's some revelation that I know how to make coffee, any idiot knows how to make coffee, it's hardly a bravura feat . . . You already asked me, in the kitchen, if I knew how to do it.

Édith (*upset*) I didn't ask you if you knew how to do it, I asked you if you'd like some help.

Alex Same thing.

Nathan (*while Alex is finishing pouring out the coffee*) Your coffee's piss.

Alex tastes it and puts his cup down with a disgusted expression.

Alex What are the others doing?

Nathan Pierre and his wife have gone for a walk. Élisa's left.

Alex Did you see her?

Nathan She came to say goodbye to us.

Alex Did you ask her to leave?

124

Nathan No.

Silence. Alex paces.

Alex The vegetable garden needs clearing, it's choked with nettles. (*to Édith*) Are there any secateurs?

Édith You want to clear the vegetable garden with secateurs?!

Alex I can't look at those woods without thinking of Dad suffocating underneath them . . . It's insane to have buried him here . . . Can't you both feel how oppressive it is? I can see his head, his nostrils full of earth, muffled birdsong . . .

Édith Stop it . . .

Nathan The secateurs are in the shed, on the table.

Alex (*turning back towards Édith*) I feel like picking some thistles, you see. Hence the secateurs. (*He leaves.*)

Pause.

Édith You remember those bouquets of thistles?

Nathan He remembers them.

Édith It's the wrong time of year . . . What shall I make for dinner? There's nothing. A tin of tuna, some rice . . .

Nathan Great.

Édith You think they'll stay this evening?

Nathan No idea.

Édith She's so exhausting . . .

Nathan She's amusing, she's lively . . .

Édith You think so?

Nathan Yes . . . I really like her.

Pause.

Édith Help me, Nathan.

Blackout.

Three

A country road. Pierre and Julienne are walking. She's taken off her coat, which she's carrying over her arm.

Julienne If I'd known it was going to be this warm, I'd have worn my gaberdine . . . You must admit, when all's said and done, you couldn't predict this in November! In any event, I can't think why I wore black, ridiculous. I was the only one in black. What are we doing this evening? You think we'll be staying for dinner?

Pierre Might be a bit insensitive to impose on them.

Julienne You see yourself driving back this evening? Couldn't we at least spend the night?

Pierre We'll see.

Julienne The countryside's so boring round here. Not a bit like Normandy. She's pretty, that Élisa. Don't you think?

Pierre Bit flat-chested.

Julienne A bit flat-chested, yes. It's the fashion. Stop. See, it's terrible, I've only got to go fifty yards and I'm gasping.

Pierre You never do any exercise; what do you expect?

Julienne No, no, it's worse than that, there's something the matter with my heart, I'm sure of it. Look, feel . . . Not like that! . . . (*She giggles.*) Really, Pierre, not in the road!

Pierre (*moving his hand around underneath her blouse*) However many layers do you have on?!

Julienne Three, not counting my coat. I put on a thermal vest just before we came out.

Pierre You must be suffocating under all that!

Julienne I am suffocating. It's the thermal vest that's really getting me down.

Pierre Take it off.

Julienne Where? Here?!

Pierre We could find a tree . . .

Julienne You see a tree anywhere?

Pierre If you had any guts, you'd take it off in the cornfield, while I keep watch in the road.

Julienne Suppose the farmer sees me?

Pierre There's no one around.

Julienne You don't know these farmers, one day Nicolas was walking across some field somewhere, and the fellow chased him in his tractor! I'll be all right, I'll be all right, stop fussing.

Pierre We'll go back if you like, you can take it off back there. At least take off your sweater.

Julienne Do you think so? . . . Oh, no, see, my arms are still cold. No, no, it's the thermal vest . . .

They half turn.

Julienne Was he married to that girl?

Pierre Who?

Julienne Alex.

Pierre No.

Julienne It's funny, three of them, and none of them ever married.

Pierre Yes.

Julienne Especially for people of that generation. It's unusual.

Pierre I married you when I was sixty-three.

Julienne You're not a very good example. Hey, look, isn't that her over there?

Pierre puts on his glasses.

Pierre Aha!

Julienne What's she doing?

Pierre Looks like she's broken down.

They set off to meet Élisa.

Four

The father's burial site.
   *Alex appears. He's holding the secateurs in one hand,
while in the other are three dry, chestnut-coloured thistle
stems. For a long moment, he looks at the earth. Finally,
he squats down. Pause.*

Alex Listen, Dad. You don't have much choice but to
listen, what with your nostrils full of earth, no more
shouting, eh? Now it's me, shouting on my own,
shouting non-stop. When I look at myself, I feel like a
little old man. I'm shouting, snapping away like a lap-
dog, there's something pinched, here, around my mouth.
When I was twelve, you slapped me once, because I was
eating a chicken leg with one hand. No warning, you
didn't even say, 'Use two hands,' you slapped me without
a word of warning. Nobody moved a muscle. I went up
to my room, sobbing like an idiot. Nathan came up –
once he'd finished eating – and said 'He's like that
because Mummy died,' my answer was: 'Fuck off, all he
has to do is die himself . . . '

   *Pierre has appeared. He's stopped, a few yards off,
silent.*

Alex Is that you?

Pierre I'm sorry . . .

Alex You paying a visit as well?

Pierre Just doing what my old legs tell me to, you know.
They lead, I follow.

Silence.

Are those thistles for him?

Alex No.

Pierre Reminds me of your mother. She used to make wonderful bouquets out of thistles. In the summer.

Alex Yes.

Pierre I'm sorry they weren't buried next to each other.

Alex This is where he wanted to be.

Pierre I know.

Alex The most selfish idea you could imagine.

Pierre There's a lot of land, you didn't have to come this far. (*He sits down on a tree stump.*) Can I stay or would you rather I went?

Alex No. Stay.

Pause.

Pierre How old are you now?

Alex Forty-three.

Pierre Forty-three . . . I saw you being born and now you're forty-three . . . When I was your age, everything seemed concentrated in the past, finished, gone . . . A kind of paradise consumed.

Alex Do you still feel that way?

Pierre No! . . . No, no, not any more . . .

Alex How old was I?

Pierre When I was your age? About twenty . . .

Alex You were living in New York . . .

Pierre Boston . . . Madly in love with an American woman. (*He laughs.*) . . . I had balls the size of grapefruit, they could have launched me into space!

Alex smiles.

Alex I remember the American woman.

Pierre Did you meet her?!

Alex No, but the American woman, Pierre's Yank, she was a family myth.

Pierre Is that right? It lasted six months, after six months she ran away to Florida with a toothpaste manufacturer.

Alex But you stayed on in America.

Pierre Three years . . . But without my American woman! There were others, but she was special . . .

Slight pause.

Alex How do you explain the fact my father never remarried?

Pierre He already had three children, why should he remarry?

Alex Did he have affairs?

Pierre Not to my knowledge. Possibly . . . (*Pause.*) Maybe with Madame Natti.

Alex Madame Natti? The chiropodist?

Pierre I couldn't prove it . . . Poor man, if he could hear me now!

Alex Madame Natti!

Pierre She was very nice, pretty little triangular face. Nathan suspected it as well.

Alex He did?!

Pierre I'm sure we were mistaken.

Alex Madame Natti . . .

Pierre You know, your father wasn't very . . . it wasn't one of his central preoccupations. He was your age when Lila died, I never knew him when he was young, but later on he always gave the impression of being kind of an ascetic.

Alex Apart from banging the chiropodist.

Pierre No! . . . Well, perhaps. I hope so!

Both of them contemplate the freshly covered earth in silence. Pause.

Pierre You know, at such melancholy moments – you'll think I'm ridiculous – what comes out of my mouth sometimes are lines of poetry . . . Stupid, isn't it?

Alex No . . .

Pierre Yes, it's stupid . . .

Pause.

Alex You know the hardest thing to understand? . . . I want to ask him to forgive me . . . When he was ill, I used to go and sit on his bed, I couldn't find the words, I wanted to take his hand one day, but he moved to rearrange his sheet or his blanket . . . I didn't persist . . . He said, 'Going all right, is it, the criticism?' 'Yes . . . ' 'Read any good books?' . . . His voice so full of bitterness! . . .

Silence.

You think I'll ever see him again? . . . You find that amusing?

133

Pierre No, no! It wasn't your question! . . . It wasn't your question that's making me smile . . .

Alex Then what is it?

Pierre Nothing . . . It's your way of . . . Your expression reminded me of something . . . Reminded me of certain expressions of yours when you were little . . . That's all.

Alex You mean at my age, you don't ask that kind of question any more, is that it?

Pierre No, no, that's not it at all!

Alex Yes, it is. You smiled with a slight air of commiseration, as if . . .

Pierre Absolutely not! I didn't smile with a slight air of anything . . . First of all, I didn't even smile, I . . . was 'repining', as they say in literature, I smiled through my repining . . . You're a real pain in the arse!

Alex What did I say? I didn't say a word . . .

Pierre And I say the first thing that comes into my head . . . I'm sorry.

Pause.

Alex You still haven't answered my question . . .

Pierre You really think I'm qualified to answer your question?

Alex You must have some opinion. Everyone has some opinion.

Pierre An opinion . . . yes.

Alex Well?

Pierre I think in a while this question of seeing him again will no longer arise . . . How's that for an opinion? . . .

Alex You mean when I'm dead?

Pierre Oh, no! Long before!

Alex But what I want is for you to tell me I will see him again! Shit, it's clear enough, it's simple enough, I want you to say to me: 'Yes. You will see him again.' That's what I need! It's grotesque of you not to understand that! That's what I need! It may be idiotic, I don't care what you think it is, but that's what I want to hear, I want someone to say to me: 'Yes! You are going to see him again!'

Silence.

Pierre I should point out that I understood what you were saying perfectly well . . .

Alex You know what he was always saying to me, the whole time! Aside from his insane desire to see me in the Académie Française. 'You have to settle down!' Settle down: that was his favourite expression . . . Can you imagine the kind of life that might conform to that idea?

Pierre When you see him again, you can ask him.

Alex Yes . . . (*He forces himself to smile.*) You understand, these are all things that have to be sorted out, otherwise . . .

Pierre Yes.

Alex Otherwise . . . I was never able to fight with him, he didn't listen to me . . . Not ever . . . I have no memory of his listening to me without getting impatient, without . . . calmly.

Pierre Yes . . .

Alex So if I never see him again . . . (*He breaks off, unable to go on.*)

Pierre You know, you don't have to say anything . . .

Alex I can't accept the idea, whatever you may think, not today, it just isn't possible . . .

Pierre Yes . . . Of course . . .

Silence.

Alex You're so bloody patient . . .

Pierre Oh, yes?

Alex Yes. You're so bloody patient.

Pierre Well, yes.

Silence.

We met Élisa down the road just now . . . Her car broke down . . . Poor thing, she was frantic. We walked back to the village, we telephoned everywhere, we couldn't find a single garage prepared to send someone out on Hallowe'en.

Alex Is she here?

Pierre Where else could she go? We brought her back, she wanted to stay sitting at the grocer's, waiting for some repair man from Gien, who'll never turn up.

Alex I haven't seen her for three years . . .

Pierre Three years . . . Long as that?

Alex Yes.

Pierre Really! . . .

Alex I wasn't expecting to see her again today . . .

Pierre Perhaps . . .

Alex No.

Pierre You don't even know what I was going to say!

Alex Yes, I do.

Pierre What was it, then?

Alex She didn't come to make me feel better, I can assure you. She didn't come for my sake . . . She came for conventional reasons. Out of respect for bourgeois tradition.

Pierre Stupid.

Alex Isn't it?

Pierre No, it's you that's stupid.

   Silence.

Alex How do you manage to be so . . .

Pierre So what?

Alex So optimistic.

Pierre Optimistic . . . I'm not sure you've chosen the appropriate word.

Alex You know what I mean. Translate it for me.

Pierre You mean in life I display a certain cheerfulness . . . Yes . . . Yes . . . But when I'm dead, no one's going to come and cry on my grave because of a chicken leg.

   Alex sobs.

   Blackout.

Five

Somewhere in the garden. Élisa, Édith and Julienne are out walking.

Julienne Who keeps it all in order? A gardener?

Édith Not any more. There used to be a gardener. Now it more or less runs itself.

Élisa I like it like this, a bit overgrown . . .

Édith Me too. After all, it's the country.

Julienne You have a big kitchen garden, it's a shame it's not being used.

Édith It's always been used. Daddy did a lot of work on it.

Julienne It's wonderful to be able to eat your own fruit. Or vegetables. Mostly vegetables, in any event!

Édith We had strawberries. And gooseberries. But the gooseberries didn't work out very well, they were sour.

Julienne I don't like gooseberries much. Unless you put them in fruit salad, with plenty of sugar.

Édith Yes . . .

Pause.

Julienne Honestly, you'd think it was the summer! I put a little woolly vest on this morning to be on the safe side, I had to take it off on the way back, I couldn't bear it any more.

Édith The grass is quite dry, it hasn't rained for days . . .
We can sit on the grass if you like?

Élisa Let's sit down.

Julienne Yes, let's sit down!

They sit down. Pause.

Édith Short hair suits you.

Élisa You think so?

Édith Shows off your pretty neck, it's very slender . . .

Élisa Nice of you to say so.

Julienne You used to have long hair?

Élisa Yes.

Édith She had a long plait hanging down.

Élisa When I first had it cut, I was practically bald,
I looked like Madame Vacher's son. It's better now.

Édith It's good like that.

Élisa Yes, it's good like that.

Silence.

Julienne While I think of it . . . (*She rummages in her
handbag.*) Here's the famous thermal vest, I stuffed it in
my handbag, otherwise I'd have forgotten it . . . I don't
think you've seen this, I brought you a photo of your
father taken at Saint-Jean during the wedding . . . Now
where is it? Ah, here it is! (*She hands the photo to
Édith.*) It's yours, obviously. (*Her voice full of sorrow.*)
I think it's really good.

Élisa It's beautiful . . .

Julienne Isn't it? Really 'warm'. 'Warm', that's the word that springs to mind.

Édith contemplates the photo.

Édith Can I keep it?

Julienne It's for you. I brought it specially.

Édith You'd think it was Nathan. The expression.

Élisa Yes, the smile . . .

Pause.

Taken during your wedding?

Julienne Yes. Taken two years ago, the date's on the back . . . I always put the date on photos, otherwise you have no idea where or when . . .

Élisa All the same, you wouldn't be likely to forget the date of your wedding!

Julienne Who knows? . . . No, of course not! But it's just one of my habits, I always put the date on documents, photos, bills, even postcards!

Élisa Do you keep them in albums?

Julienne Postcards? No!

Élisa Photos.

Julienne Oh, yes. Of course I do . . . Don't you?

Élisa No.

Julienne Don't you either, Édith?

Édith Yes, I do . . .

Julienne I have six or seven at least. Children, grand-children . . . It's my hoarding instinct, like an ant.

They smile.
  Pause.

Édith Do you still see your first husband, Julienne?

Julienne My first husband's dead, poor man, he had a heart attack when he was thirty-five.

Édith I'm sorry, I had no idea.

Julienne Don't be sorry, how could you have known? After that I married a dentist, whom I divorced eight years ago. We stayed on good terms, we see each other occasionally. When I married Pierre, he even sent me a congratulatory telegram.

Élisa Three husbands. If I may say so, you've done the work for all of us!

Julienne On my eighteenth birthday, a hypersensitive clairvoyant predicted I would become a nun. I was no beauty, but even so! So I launched myself, you might say, on a counter-offensive . . .

Élisa And won.

Julienne (*modestly*) Ultimately, yes.

  Silence.
    Édith stares into the distance, overcome by some private suffering. Élisa and Julienne secretly watch her, not daring to say any more.

Édith When I was little, I used to make necklaces out of daisies. Daisy-chain crowns on my head . . . In spring, the ground around here is covered in them.

Élisa Do you still see Jean?

Édith More or less . . . I'm talking about daisy chains and you're thinking about Jean.

Élisa (*smiling*) No . . .

Édith My perennial lover . . .

Pause.

You know what Daddy used to say: 'Your greatest
success in life, the only act you can congratulate yourself
on, is not to have married Jean!' . . . He used to call him
Mr Tsetse Fly . . . (*She smiles.*) . . . It was so stupid! So
stupid that after a while we couldn't help laughing . . .
(*She can't help laughing.*) . . . 'Invite Mr Tsetse Fly, he'll
put us to sleep!'

She laughs. Julienne and Élisa follow suit.

Daddy's dead, but I still have Jean. And Jean's going to
London . . . I'm a dried-up old apple.

Silence.

Julienne If you're a dried-up old apple, what am I? . . .

Édith You have children, you have grandchildren, you
have a husband, a family . . . You wear make-up, you get
dressed up . . .

Julienne Well, nothing's stopping you wearing make-up
or getting dressed up! . . .

Édith For whom?

Julienne For anyone! For everyone . . . For yourself!

Édith I'd want it to be for someone, to make myself
beautiful for someone . . .

Julienne I'm sorry, Édith, but your reasoning is
backwards. Wear make-up, get dressed up, and the
someone will turn up within the hour! . . . (*to Élisa*)
Am I talking nonsense, dear?

Élisa No . . .

Édith I spent the night with a man. One night . . . My boss, nothing could be more banal . . . One evening, I waited for him by his car, I said to him, 'I want to stay with you tonight' . . . 'All night?' he answered. I said, 'Yes' . . . (*Pause.*) I had no make-up, nothing . . . I was just as I am now . . .

Silence.

Élisa What happened?

Édith I don't know why I'm telling you this now.

Élisa Tell us anyway . . .

Édith We went to his house. He offered me a drink. He got undressed and we went to bed as if it was the most natural thing in the world . . .

Pause.

I cried . . . We spent a moment pressed against each other and then he withdrew and I retreated to the far side of the bed . . . He said, 'What's the matter?' He leant over me, he ran his hand through my hair, he touched my cheek, he said, 'Come here' . . . He lifted me up and I went back and buried myself against him . . . He said, 'What's the matter? Why are you crying? Is it my fault?' I wanted to say yes and I said no, because what his question meant was, 'Wasn't I what you wanted?' and in fact he had been, down to the least little gesture, with all his slightly weary ardour, exactly what I wanted . . .

Pause.

Élisa Did you see him again?

Édith Yes, at the office. Nothing else . . . Then he left.

Silence.

At thirty-nine . . . I was thirty-nine at the time . . . I was
no lover . . . I didn't know what to do . . . This man, if
he'd looked at me, perhaps I might have been able to
make myself more attractive . . .

Pause.

During the burial this morning – I haven't been able
to think about anything else all day – I imagined him
appearing behind a tree . . . Staying slightly to one
side and never taking his eyes off me . . . All women
tell the same stories. There's no philosophical system
behind it . . .

Élisa Are you sure? . . .

Slight pause.

Édith Why did you come?

Élisa You know why I came.

Édith No . . .

Élisa Too bad.

Édith When I saw you arriving, I thought you must be
crazy . . .

Élisa Do you still think that?

Édith Yes . . .

Élisa Then why ask the question?

Édith (*to Julienne, who in spite of her embarrassment
and a growing incomprehension is forcing herself to look
neutral*) This woman, my dear Julienne, has driven both
my brothers crazy.

Élisa Don't exaggerate.

Édith To distraction, then, if you prefer, with love! . . .
Don't make that face at me, I'm not blind, you know . . .

Élisa You're wrong. I wish you were right, but you're wrong . . . (*to Julienne*) If you'll allow me to set the record straight: I simply lived with Alex and it was I who loved Nathan 'to distraction'. There . . . You must admit that's something quite different.

Julienne smiles politely.

Édith You were his mistress?

Élisa For one night . . .

Édith Does Alex know?

Élisa No. I don't think so . . . One night of love and then separation . . . (*She smiles.*) Like you and your boss . . . And you, Julienne, don't you have some night to tell us about? May I call you Julienne?

Julienne No . . . I mean, yes, obviously you can call me Julienne! . . . but I don't have a night . . . I mean, I don't have a night, er . . . of course there were nights, but I don't have that particular kind of a night . . . I'm expressing myself horribly badly all of a sudden. (*She brings a handkerchief out of her handbag, very jittery.*)

Édith We're being very rude to you.

Julienne Oh, no, not at all.

Élisa She's right, I'm sorry.

Julienne No, there's no reason to be. I'm not on the scrap-heap yet, even if I look as if I am!

Élisa That's not what I meant! Besides, that's not at all the impression you give.

Julienne I was joking. (*Slight pause.*) I'd like to make a small comment, Édith, even though my position as involuntary audience perhaps doesn't entitle me to this observation, but I find it entirely natural, entirely natural on a day like today, for you to clutch at certain memories. Clutch is an ugly word, that's not what I meant to say . . . What's the word for bumping into something . . . Bump . . . Collide?

Édith It's done me good to talk. I'm not thinking about it any more, already.

> *Silence.*
> *Nathan appears, carrying a shopping-basket, from which carrots and leek stems protrude. He stops and takes a slight pause, surprised.*

Nathan You came back?

Élisa My car broke down. They're going to come and fix it about six o'clock . . . You didn't see it?

Nathan I wasn't on that road, I've just come back from Dampierre. What's wrong with it?

Élisa You're asking me?!

Nathan You want me to take a look at it?

Élisa You know something about cars?

Nathan No. Nothing whatsoever.

Élisa The grocer says it's the automatic gearbox.

Nathan (*smiling*) Of course, he's an expert, Monsieur Vacher! . . . I've brought the makings of an enormous *pot-au-feu*, will you come with me, ladies?

> *They leave, following Nathan.*
> *Blackout.*

Six

The terrace.
  *Nathan appears, immediately followed by Édith,
Julienne and Élisa. He puts down the basket and empties
its contents on to the table.*

Nathan Leeks, carrots, shoulder of beef and marrow-
bones, parsley, tomatoes . . .

Édith You don't put tomatoes in a *pot-au-feu*.

Nathan We'll put them in just this once . . . gherkins,
potatoes and . . . turnips! Is that all right? I hope you're
staying for dinner?

Julienne Love to, if Pierre has no objection.

Nathan Where is he?

Julienne With your brother somewhere, I imagine. I can
start peeling the vegetables, if you like?

Nathan We can all peel them together, can't we, out
here? Make the most of the sun.

Édith I'll go and put the meat on. I'll bring some knives.
(*She leaves, taking with her the meat, the parsley and the
box of gherkins.*)

Nathan (*to Élisa*) Are you staying?

Élisa No . . .

Nathan Don't be silly, how are you planning to get
away?

Élisa I don't know. If the car really is buggered, I'll take the train. There must be a train from Gien.

Julienne Stay, we'll take you back.

Élisa I don't think so, thanks . . .

Nathan Will you help us to peel the vegetables anyway?

Élisa (*smiling*) Yes, of course . . . You've bought enough for a regiment.

Nathan I have no sense of proportion . . . I asked the woman to give me all the necessary ingredients for a *pot-au-feu*, it was she who put the tomatoes in. You really don't put tomatoes in a *pot-au-feu*?

Élisa In principle, no.

Julienne We'll make a little salad, that'd be nice.

Nathan There we are.

Édith returns with some sheets of newspaper, some knives, a colander and two salad bowls. She puts everything on the table next to the vegetables.

Édith I'll put the water on to boil, I'll be back. (*She sets off again.*)

Élisa, Nathan and Julienne spread the paper out on the table, sit down and start peeling.

Julienne You don't have a peeler? Although it's just as quick to do it with an ordinary knife.

Nathan Want me to go and have a look?

Julienne No, no, don't bother. I'm just being fussy, I'll be perfectly fine with this.

Pierre appears, followed by Alex.

Pierre What's this? What's this?

Julienne Are you going to come and give me a hand, darling?

Pierre Is that wise?

Alex What is it?

Nathan A *pot-au-feu*.

Pierre sits at the table. Alex remains standing, motionless.

Pierre (*to Élisa*) I'm a killer at this sort of thing. I take scalps!

Alex (*to Élisa*) Has your car broken down?

Élisa Yes . . .

Alex Did you call the garage?

Élisa Yes . . . someone's coming for it about six o'clock.

Alex What's the matter with it?

Nathan Monsieur Vacher says it's the automatic gear-box!

Alex Really! . . . You have an automatic?

Élisa (*smiling*) Yes.

Alex Good . . . Practical in town, is it?

Élisa Yes . . .

Alex Practical. Good . . . (*Pause.*) Where's Édith?

Nathan In the kitchen. She's coming.

Alex Good, well . . . let's get peeling! . . . (*He sits at the table and grasps a turnip.*)

Silence. Édith arrives.

Édith Ah, you're all here!

Pierre Personally, I'm just supervising!

Édith Can you make some room for me, next to you, in the sun?

Pierre Yes, here, come!

Julienne I'm repeating what I said this morning, but, in any event, I've never seen weather like this in November!

Alex This turnip is rotten.

Julienne I must admit, these are not best-quality turnips. (*to Nathan*) It's not your fault!

Nathan I can't say I feel particularly guilty.

Julienne In any case you're doing that like a real professional!

Nathan You think so?

Alex My brother's a great professional, Julienne. At everything and in every way. He's what I would call a professional personified.

Nathan This is not a compliment, you understand.

Alex Why? It is a compliment . . . (*He picks up a second turnip.*) Words are the only things which change over time . . . When I was a child, all my heroes looked like Nathan. Sinbad, D'Artagnan, my favourite Tom Sawyer, all Nathan . . . The radiant, invincible Nathan, the one exemplary being . . . Rotten as well. Completely! . . . (*He throws the turnip aside and picks up a potato.*) You know he was giving piano concerts when he was ten. In the drawing room. The whole family used to listen religiously.

Julienne Do you still play?

Nathan I still play, but I don't give recitals any more!

Alex Ah, yes! . . . More's the pity . . . At one time, I used to play the flute . . .

Laughter.

No, no, it's true! The 'Kena' . . . A sort of hollow piece of bamboo, with holes, I bought it in the Metro. It was my Cordillera period, with my llama-wool bonnet from the Andes.

Édith I don't remember hearing you play.

Alex You don't? Well, neither do I. I never managed to get a peep out of it.

Pierre And that's what you call playing the flute.

Alex Certainly. You put on a record, say the Machucambos, and you play along, in front of the mirror . . .

Nathan In a red poncho . . .

Alex Yes, and that little cagoule that suited me so well . . . Dad conducted the world's great orchestras that way.

Élisa In a poncho?

Alex No. In his pyjamas . . . Tell me, do these vegetables reduce in the stock? You've got enough here for six months!

Édith We don't have to put them all in.

Alex Are you staying to dinner? What I mean is, are you staying the night?

Pierre If it's all right with everyone, I'd just as soon leave tomorrow morning.

Édith Your room's made up, you could even stay till Monday.

Pierre No, no . . .

Julienne I didn't bring my toothbrush or my nightie.

Pierre Great!

Julienne Listen to him! . . .

Nathan You'll find everything you need here.

Julienne Thanks very much.

Élisa I need to telephone the station at Gien.

Édith It's Saturday . . . There's a train at eight.

Nathan I'll come with you.

Élisa Thank you . . .

Édith Stop! That's enough, no point in peeling the rest, otherwise I won't know what to do with it.

She gets up and starts clearing up. Élisa, Julienne and Pierre follow suit. Nathan leaves the table and moves away to light a cigarette. Only Alex stays seated.

Julienne (*to Nathan*) You know what you've forgotten? Not that it matters: an onion!

Nathan Oh, yes, sorry.

Julienne I'm teasing, but it does give it a bit of flavour!

Nathan Yes, yes.

Toing and froing. They disperse, carrying vegetables and peelings into the house. Alex and Nathan remain. Pause.

Alex . . . 'It does give it a bit of flavour!'

Édith reappears to collect the salad bowls.

Nathan Do you need me any more?

Édith No, no, there's nothing left to do . . .

She grabs the knife and the potato which Alex is still whittling away at and leaves. Nathan wanders away down the garden. Alex is alone.

Blackout.

Seven

The father's burial site.
  Nathan is motionless, his hands in his pockets. There are thistle stalks on the ground and, not far off, the secateurs.
  Silence.
  Soundlessly, and as if not daring to approach, Élisa appears. There's a long pause before the dialogue.

Nathan Two weeks ago, I went into his room, he couldn't get up any more . . . He asked me to bring him the record player and the loudspeakers, those were the expressions he used . . . I set it up beside his bed. He wanted to listen to the *Arioso* of Opus 110, Beethoven's penultimate sonata, only that passage . . . We listened in silence, he raised a finger like that, so I wouldn't speak. I was sitting on his bed. There's a fugue in the middle, then the theme starts up again . . . When the record was finished, he said to me: 'I'm convinced we're going to meet.' I asked him: 'Who?' 'Beethoven, the exemplary genius . . . A man who provides you with that kind of intuition, surely you don't think he can be dead!' Unlike Alex, I'm very happy he's buried here.

  Silence.

Élisa Whose decision was it?

Nathan His. He didn't want cemeteries and funerals . . . Since he retired, he's been living here.

Élisa Even when he was ill?

Nathan Yes. He had a full-time nurse.

Pause.

Élisa And Alex?

Nathan Alex? . . .

Élisa Was he with him?

Nathan He came to see him . . . Often at the wrong time, poor sod. He'd bring him books when Dad wasn't able to read, and he moved in, at the end, when the old man couldn't recognise anybody any more . . . You've changed.

Élisa Aged.

Nathan No. Yes, perhaps.

Silence.

Élisa Are you still at Nanterre?

Nathan No. I've been called to the bar in Paris.

Élisa Ah . . .

Pause.

Nathan And you?

Élisa Nothing special . . .

Nathan Meaning?

Élisa Nothing. My life hasn't changed.

Pause.

Nathan You still living at the other end of the world?

Élisa Yes.

Nathan Rue Saint-Bernard.

Élisa Yes.

Nathan Good . . .

Élisa smiles.

It was nice what you said to me.

Élisa Thanks. Is that the word? . . .

Nathan What do you want me to say?

Élisa Nothing . . .

Nathan Your car breaking down, it's like something out of a novel.

Élisa I swear it's true.

Nathan I believe you. If you ask me, it's him, up there in Heaven, who's contrived to bugger the motor around a bit.

Élisa Don't be ridiculous.

Nathan I'm not. He did it to give me pleasure . . .

Pause.

Élisa It gives you pleasure that I'm here?

Nathan What do you think? . . . Alex has forgotten the secateurs.

Silence.
Nathan picks up the secateurs and puts them in his pocket.

Why did you come?

Élisa Now?

Nathan Today.

Élisa You'd do better to ask me how I found the strength to come . . . I've never done anything so contrary to reason.

Silence.

You want me to leave you?

Nathan No. I don't want you to leave me . . . (*Pause.*) You're more of a forbidden fruit than ever, Élisa. But today I don't want you to leave me . . . (*Pause.*) You know what I'm thinking? Something equally contrary to reason . . . That I'd like to have you. Here. On top of his grave . . . To banish one kind of pain with another. (*She goes right up to him.*)

Élisa Let me be your pain, Nathan . . .

He kisses her passionately and starts to undress her.

Blackout.

Eight

The terrace.
  Alex, still at the table.
  Julienne appears, in a great rush.

Julienne Where's Élisa?

Alex She's fucking my brother.

Julienne I beg your pardon?!

Alex She's in the process of fucking my brother.

Julienne I don't understand!

Alex Yes, you do, Julienne, you understand very well.
You're not deaf, are you?

Julienne But where?!

Alex Ha! Ha! Ha! . . . What a wonderful question! Ha!
Ha! . . . Still, you're very quick on your feet!

Julienne That's not what I meant to say! . . . I meant
you're here . . . given that you're here and I've just come
out of the house . . . oh, damn it!

  She leaves, very flustered. Édith arrives.

Édith Where's Élisa?

Alex No idea.

Édith You didn't see her come out?

Alex Yes, she went that way . . .

Édith Pierre's on the phone with the garage, they can't
send anyone before Monday morning!

Alex shrugs his shoulders.

What can we do?

Alex Call someone else . . .

Édith It's the only place available. Anyway, no one does repairs on a Sunday! . . . What can we do? Shall we agree to Monday? And if we leave tomorrow evening, who are we going to leave the keys with?

Alex Do what you like, I couldn't give a flying fuck.

Édith We could leave them with Vacher, he knows where the car is. He's not closed on Monday morning, is he?

Alex I don't know. I don't give a fuck.

Édith Thanks for your help . . . (*She leaves.*)

Alex Can't she climb out of her own pile of shit?! . . . Why's she getting on our tits with her clapped-out old heap?!!

He stays seated for a moment, alone. Then gets up, turns and moves a few steps towards the woods. Pierre appears.

Pierre Where are you going?

Alex Mm?!

Pierre It's going to rain.

Alex You think so? Yes . . .

Pierre Stormy weather. That's why it's been so warm.

Alex Yes . . .

Pause.

Pierre Care for a cigarillo?

Alex You smoke cigarillos?

Pierre Once every six months . . . (*He offers the packet to Alex, who helps himself.*) Present from the concierge. Spanish cigarillos. What do you think? (*Alex coughs.*) Strong, eh?

Alex (*coughing and laughing*) It's disgusting!

Pierre Yes.

Alex It's like . . .

Pierre Cheese. *Pont-l'évêque*. Tastes like *Pont-l'évêque* . . . I mean, you get used to it . . .

Alex When are you leaving?

Pierre Tomorrow morning. Is that a problem for you?

Alex No, no . . . Can you think of anything more lugubrious than the country in the autumn? . . . The silence . . . Nothing moving . . . I hate the country . . . If it was up to me, I'd sell the whole lot . . . Tomorrow.

He moves around, smoking his cigarillo. Pierre stays still.

Nathan adores the country.

Pierre You're very unfair to Nathan.

Alex In what way? Because I say he likes the country?

Pierre Among other things . . .

Alex You think that's a character flaw?

Pierre I don't, no.

Alex Nathan goes for walks, he tramps around on his own for hours . . . (*Pause.*) He meditates, among the trees.

Pierre Whereas you shout yourself hoarse in the turbulent maelstrom of life . . .

Alex smiles. Slight pause.

Everything you do badly, he does well . . . Everything you dislike makes him happy . . . To judge from what you say, he's the most respectable man on earth, and the most inhuman . . .

Alex Inhuman? No . . .

Pierre Yes. Talented, deep, uninfluenceable . . . all your rattlesnake compliments . . . no one can stand up against that, believe me.

Alex (*after a pause, as if getting his breath back*) You're on very good form, Pierrot, but you don't understand what you're talking about . . .

Pierre Nothing new about that, as you know . . . Are you cold?

Alex Freezing.

Pierre You want to go in?

Alex No.

Silence.

Three years ago, Élisa left me. At that time, everybody thought I was an idiot. A blind idiot. He undertook never to see her again. Out of friendship towards me, I imagine . . . He stood aside . . . just as he gave up music, just as he gave up his brilliance, his streak of madness, his heroism . . . I've certainly never loved anyone as much as him. If Nathan died, you can't imagine how lonely I'd be . . . as lonely as he is today, perhaps . . . But once again he says nothing. He goes shopping for dinner . . . He comes back with a ton of vegetables, and everybody sits peeling them in the sun because of him, solely because of him . . .

Édith appears. Silence.

All right?

Édith Yes . . . (*Pause.*) Who were you talking about?

Alex Nathan.

Édith What were you saying?

Alex You like the country as well, don't you?

Édith What a strange question!

Alex You don't think it's lugubrious?

Édith Today, perhaps.

Pierre With this sudden light . . .

Édith It's going to rain.

Pierre Exactly what we were saying.

Édith Be so good as not to take me for a complete fool.

Pierre What do you mean? It's true. It's exactly what we were saying.

Pause.

Alex Have you sorted out the car business?

Pierre Yes . . . I told the man to come and fetch it on Monday. What's my wife doing?

Édith Watching TV.

Pierre What's on?

Édith I don't know. Some variety show, I don't know . . .

Pierre Good . . . I didn't even know you had a telly here, is that new?

Édith It's been here about a year . . . We had it put in for Daddy.

Pierre Oh, yes, of course . . .

Silence.

Édith Everything's on the stove, at last. I put everything in three big pots, we'll eat the leftovers tomorrow . . . Can I have one of those little cigars?

Alex I wouldn't recommend it.

Édith Why?

Pierre Don't listen to him. (*He offers the packet to Édith.*) Here you are.

Édith Are they not good?

Alex They're out of the ordinary . . .

Édith (*smoking*) I don't mind.

They watch her smoking.

Don't look at me like that! (*She laughs.*) It looks like you've given me poison and now you're waiting for me to die!

Alex You're not far wrong . . .

Nathan appears, followed by Élisa. He's holding the secateurs and the thistle stalks cut by Alex.
Silence.

Nice walk?

Nathan Did you cut these?

Alex I might have left them there on purpose . . .

Nathan And the secateurs? . . . I brought everything, to be on the safe side.

Slight pause.

Alex (*to Élisa*) You were together?

163

Nathan Yes. Why?

Alex I'm allowed to ask a question. Why say why?

Pierre (*to Élisa*) I had the garage on the phone.

Élisa What time is it?

Pierre Calm down, just calm down! He can't come this evening. We agreed on Monday morning.

Édith Since no one will be here, I've said we'll leave the keys at the grocer's . . . Unless you can think of another solution?

Élisa I'm sorry to have been such a nuisance . . .

Pierre The only nuisance is to you! Not to mention you'll have to come back to collect it.

Élisa Yes.

Pierre Let's hope it's nothing too serious.

Élisa Yes . . .

Alex She's no longer with us . . .

Élisa What?!

Alex You're no longer with us, Élisa . . . Am I wrong?

Nathan We're all a bit distracted today. Aren't we?

Alex Absolutely!

Nathan There are times one couldn't give a damn what's happened to one's car . . .

Alex Yes, personally I couldn't give a tuppenny damn!

Nathan Well, she feels the same way.

Alex Well, great! . . . (*Pause.*) Not very nice for Pierre and Édith!

Édith (*to Élisa*) Don't listen to him.

Élisa They're speaking for me, I haven't said a word . . .

Nathan What's become of my *pot-au-feu*?

Édith It's cooking.

Nathan It's going to rain . . .

Élisa (*to Pierre*) Where's your wife?

Pierre Inside. Watching TV.

Nathan Perhaps we should join her?

Pierre Very good idea. Providing we switch the thing off . . . (*to Élisa*) Will you come with me?

> *Élisa goes over to Pierre, who leads her away towards the house. Nathan is about to follow them when Édith intercepts him.*

Édith Could you stay a minute? There's something I want to say to you . . .

Alex Am I in the way?

Édith Yes, please, I won't be long.

> *Alex hesitates. He takes a few steps, then turns back.*

Alex (*to Édith*) By the way . . . I learned something about Dad just now, I thought it might amuse you to know about it as well . . .

Édith What?

Alex Ask him . . .

> *He goes up to Nathan and whispers a word in his ear. Nathan smiles.*

(*to Édith*) Everyone has his secrets . . . (*He moves away.*) I'll be in my room. If anyone needs me.

Nathan (*flourishing the thistles*) What shall I do with these?

Alex Throw them away.

He disappears. Édith and Nathan are alone.

Édith Tell me.

Nathan You first . . .

Édith It's raining . . .

Nathan No . . .

Édith Yes, I felt a drop . . . Will you help me put the chairs away?

Nathan What's the matter?

Pause.

Édith You were with Élisa?

Nathan Yes.

Édith She went to find you?

Nathan Yes!

Édith Alex said to Julienne that you were fucking Élisa. I'm quoting word for word . . .

Nathan Is that what you wanted to say to me?

Édith Yes.

Nathan So?

Édith What do you mean, 'so'?

Nathan So?

Édith So, you think that's normal?

Nathan What do you mean by normal? Is it the phrase that's disturbing you or the idea it implies?

Édith You're a monster . . .

Nathan Listen, Édith, so far today has passed off without upheavals, if I may say so . . . Will you leave those chairs alone! . . . We're civilised people, we observe the rules, everyone holds their breath, there's no tragedy . . . And why exactly? I don't know, but that's the way it is. You and I collaborate in this effort for dignity . . . We're discreet, 'elegant', we behave perfectly . . . It's not that Alex is less civilised, but his pride lives somewhere else . . . Somewhere else.

Édith Why do you defend him?

Nathan I'm not defending him . . . If he comes and tells poor Julienne that I'm fucking Élisa, that's part of his nature, but you repeating it to me, off to one side like at school, like a little girl, you being so concerned about it, today, well, that I don't understand.

   Silence.

Édith I repeated it to you so that you'd know Alex's state of mind . . . She's crazy to have come today.

Nathan No.

Édith Yes.

Nathan No, I said. You repeated it to me out of curiosity. Because you had a suspicion . . . (*He comes up to her and takes her in his arms.*) . . . Mm? . . . (*He kisses her and tenderly strokes her hair.*)

Édith Do you still love her?

Nathan That's what you wanted to say to me.

   Édith moves away. She looks around, confused. The weather's changed. Everything is grey.

Shall we go in?

Édith What were you supposed to tell me about Daddy?

Nathan (*hesitates before speaking*) You remember Madame Natti?

Édith The chiropodist?

Nathan Yes . . .

Édith What about her?

Nathan Well, it seems that Dad's chiropody sessions were perhaps . . . and this is purely supposition . . . not entirely devoted to his feet . . . You see, after all, we're not really changing the subject.

Édith Daddy . . . ?!

Nathan Daddy.

Édith With that woman . . .

Nathan She was pretty . . .

Édith She was at least thirty years younger . . .

Nathan In which case, he wasn't doing too badly . . .

Édith Did you know?

Nathan More or less.

Édith Did he tell you?

Nathan No . . . I was at his place one day, in the Rue Pierre-Demours, and Madame Natti arrived, she set up her little washbowl and laid out her scissors . . . and I left. I'd forgotten my glasses, I went back ten minutes later . . . I rang, rang again, and finally Dad arrived, slightly dishevelled, to open the door, wrapped in that yellow oilskin, you know, the yellow oilskin which hung in the front hall this last hundred years, I thought it was somewhat peculiar indoor wear . . . He gave me back my glasses through the door, without letting me back in . . .

Édith You didn't ask him anything?

Nathan Yes. To fetch my glasses.

Édith Why didn't you tell us?

Nathan makes an evasive gesture. Pause.

Poor man . . .

Nathan Poor man? . . . Why?

Édith Because.

They stand there a moment, both motionless.

Blackout.

Nine

Inside the house.
Armchairs, a low table. A small sideboard. Élisa,
Julienne and Pierre are sitting down.

Pierre I was living in a little studio on Rue Lepic. At that time I hadn't a penny, but I did have a very rich mistress, the wife of a Dieppe lawyer who had an office in Paris. In short, the fellow travelled a lot, and one year in particular she found herself on her own over Christmas. I wasn't doing anything special, bits and pieces, and she suggested we go and spend a week in Megève. A lovers' jaunt. Why not? She says to me: 'Here's the money, you make the bookings, train tickets, hotel and so on.' I take the money and I go to a travel agent's in Rue . . . can't remember, anyway, not far from the Opéra. I book the hotel, I book the sleeper, I pay and I leave . . .

Alex appears.

Alex Keep going!

Pierre I'm telling the Paillot story, you know the one . . .

Alex Go on, go on . . .

As Pierre continues, Alex remains on his feet.

Pierre So, where was I? . . . Yes, so, I'm leaving. I walk down the street, I'm about to take a bus to the Opéra. I'm waiting, and as the bus arrives, who should I see getting off? Paillot. An old classmate I used to see from time to time, very funny, very nice – still a friend by the way – and completely broke! . . . Hello! All right? How are you? He asks me what I'm doing and I tell him I'm off to Megève the next day. Whereupon, er . . . he wasn't doing anything, he was a bit down, he says to me, 'It's wonderful, Megève,' and suddenly I'm saying to him: 'Well, you know . . . ' and bringing out the envelope from the travel agent's . . . 'It's all here, everything booked for two, travel, hotel, demi-pension, if you're free, let's you and me bugger off tomorrow evening!' He looks at me, he says, 'What about the girl?' 'Don't worry, I just won't call her, out of sight, out of mind, anyway she's starting to piss me off.' And away we went!

Alex And what happened?

Pierre Well, nothing, what happened, Megève, the snow, wonderful . . .

Alex I thought she chased after you later to get her money back . . .

Pierre Yes, well, more or less . . . you know, she never did get it back!

Julienne It's monstrous! Are we supposed to think that story's funny?

Alex Why is it monstrous?

Julienne When I think of that poor woman all on her own in Paris! (*She laughs.*)

Pierre See, you're laughing.

Julienne I shouldn't be.

Pierre Are you shocked, Élisa?

Élisa Not at all! I think it's a very funny story. And so does Julienne, which proves it.

Julienne No, what's shocking is he never paid her back. He could have got her a present . . . At least sent her a bunch of flowers! A huge bunch!

Pierre I nearly sent her a postcard when we were down there, maybe I should have.

Julienne Don't make yourself out to be even more awful than you are . . . (*to Élisa*) He thinks you'll find him attractive, poor dear!

Alex Élisa's very susceptible to this sort of humour. She likes cynical and immoral men.

Pierre Steady on!

Alex Not you, poor old Pierrot, you're a choirboy. (*He moves towards the imaginary window.*) It's raining . . .

Pierre Are they still outside?

Pause.

Julienne Strange how changeable the weather is!

Élisa Yes . . .

Alex Have you ever seen a map of the world designed by a Russian? Russia is in the centre and we're stuck up the top in a sort of deep gully . . . It's fascinating!

Pierre May we know why you're suddenly talking about this?

Alex Because I'm looking out at the country.

Nathan arrives, drenched.

Julienne God, you're soaked!

Nathan It's nothing, nothing at all, does you good.

Pierre Where's your sister?

Nathan Gone upstairs to change.

Pierre You find us in the middle of a geography lesson!

Alex Philosophy . . .

Pierre Philosophy!

Nathan May I join in?

Alex smiles. Pause.

Nathan Well . . . all right, too bad!

Élisa You ought to change, you'll catch cold.

Nathan No, no, it'll dry . . .

Pierre I told them the Paillot story! . . .

Nathan (*to Julienne*) Hadn't you heard it?

Julienne No!

Pierre She was appalled.

Julienne Absolutely not! In any event, I don't see why I should be appalled!

Nathan It's dark . . . it's miserable here. Aren't you drinking anything? Not even a cup of tea?

Édith appears.

Édith I got changed, I was drenched . . .

Alex What about a little game to cheer us all up a bit? Mm? Monopoly, Scrabble, we have everything.

Nathan Draughts, chess . . .

Édith You're not going to play a game? No one wants to play a game!

Nathan Cluedo . . .

Alex Cluedo! Ha! Ha! The silliest bloody game in the world! . . . What made you think of that?!

Nathan I'm afraid Julienne might not know the rules.

Alex Of course she does, Colonel Mustard . . .

Nathan Professor Plum . . .

Julienne Mrs Peacock . . .

Alex There you are!

Pierre You know this game?

Julienne Of course I do. What do you take me for, an idiot? You forget I have two grandchildren.

Nathan And you play Cluedo with them?

Julienne Cluedo, snakes and ladders, snap . . .

Édith How old are they?

Julienne Three and seven. Of course, I only play with the older one. The little one's only just started to talk. He says, 'Daddy', he says . . . Not that it means much, because children are more . . . I mean, at the end of the day, children who are late starters are often the most talkative!

Alex Then you must have started pretty late, did you?

Élisa Alex!

Alex What?! . . . What is it, Élisa?

Élisa Nothing . . .

Alex Yes! You said 'Alex!' What is it?

Silence.

Élisa Calm down . . .

Alex I'm quite calm. Do I seem agitated?

Édith Right, that's enough now . . .

Alex What do you mean, 'that's enough'? What's going on? You're really pissing me off!

Nathan You must be a late starter as well . . . Although in your case the evidence isn't very conclusive.

Alex In any event! . . . Oh, Julienne, you absolutely have to explain to me the meaning of that phrase! You use it so often, you've infected me with it what's more, but I still can't grasp the, what should I call it, its 'etymology' . . .

Pierre That's a shaming admission for a literary critic.

Alex That's why I absolutely have to find out about it!

Élisa Stop it, Alex . . .

Alex You want me to stop it?

Élisa Yes.

Alex Then I'll stop it.

   Pause.

Édith Go and make us a coffee, since you're so good at it.

Nathan No, herbal tea!

Alex Herbal tea? Drop of herbal tea, Julienne? I was joking. I was joking! A drop of herbal tea for everyone?

Édith Go away!

Alex I'm going. (*He leaves.*) I'm going.

   Silence.

Nathan He was joking, Julienne . . . You mustn't take him seriously.

Julienne It's nice of you, but I don't think your brother likes me at all.

All He does!

Julienne (*on the brink of tears*) No, no, but it doesn't matter, it doesn't matter at all . . .

Édith Julienne, he's not his normal self today . . .

Julienne I know, I know that! Naturally, you're all very upset today, and I'm just stuck here like a . . . (*She's crying.*) Pierre insisted I came, but I'm like a stranger, I'm not really part of this family . . .

Élisa If there's someone here who's not part of this family, it's me, Julienne. Not you. You're their aunt, of course you're part of the family . . .

Julienne (*in tears*) He said things to me just now . . . As if I was some brute beast . . .

Nathan What did he say to you?

Julienne Nothing . . . He was making fun of me, that's all . . . Don't tell him, Édith, I beg of you!

Édith I'll go and look for him.

She leaves.

Julienne No! Why's she going to look for him? Leave him in peace, poor man . . .

Pierre What a day, my dears!

Julienne I'm so sorry . . . I'm so sorry, I'm ridiculous . . .

Nathan You have no reason to be sorry.

Julienne You're doing everything you can to . . . And I just start crying! . . . Like an idiot . . . (*She sobs.*) That's all I can find to do!

Édith comes back, followed by Alex. Alex stops in front of Julienne, not saying anything.

(*to Alex*) It's not your fault . . . It's all over. I'm sorry, everybody.

*Alex takes hold of Julienne's arm and raises her up.
When she's on her feet, he takes her in his arms,
embraces her and holds her for a time, pressed against
him.*

*When he lets her go, Julienne's face is streaked with
tears.*

Pause.

Pierre (*to Alex*) You wouldn't have something to drink a
bit stronger than herbal tea?

Alex Yes . . . Of course! . . .

Élisa Can I come with you?

Alex Nowhere to go, it's all here.

*Assisted by Nathan, he opens the door of the
sideboard and brings out some bottles, which he puts
on the low table.*

Nathan You're spoilt for choice, my friends . . . I
particularly recommend the green bottle. Distilled from
Hungarian artichokes . . .

Pierre It's a liqueur!

Nathan It's whatever you want it to be. You can take
it with water, or ice, you can poison your wife with it!

Pierre No, we'll let her live!

Nathan Taste it, you'll see.

Pierre Is it disgusting?

Nathan A client brought it back for me. It's been there
fifteen years.

Pierre Go on, give me a whisky!

Nathan Julienne?

Julienne A drop of port . . .

Alex pours it for her.

Thanks. When. You're very kind.

Nathan Élisa?

Élisa Give me a taste of the Hungarian stuff.

Pierre Ah, I was sure of it! I was sure someone would taste it and I was sure it was going to be you!

Élisa Why, do I look like someone who drinks artichoke liqueur?

Pierre You look like a pioneer! Especially your eyes . . . You have adventurous pupils!

Édith What are you talking about!

Pierre No. It's true. You like taking risks. You don't like anyone dictating the way you behave. Am I wrong?

Élisa (*smiling*) In fact, I don't have the feeling I'm taking much of a risk!

Nathan (*handing her the glass*) Don't speak too soon . . .

Élisa (*raising her glass*) We shall see what we shall see . . .

Édith What about me, you're not offering me a drink?

Alex What would you like?

Édith White port. (*to Pierre*) You're drinking it like that? Wouldn't you like some ice?

Pierre No, no, don't worry. This is perfect.

Alex and Nathan serve themselves. Élisa tastes the artichoke liqueur.

Nathan Well?

Élisa . . . It's sweet, full of nostalgia and red pepper . . .

She empties the glass.

Nathan Another?

Élisa Yes . . . You only just covered the bottom of the glass.

He pours some more for her. Élisa smiles at Pierre.
Pause.
Sound of the rain falling.

Pierre
'O pallid seasons, queens who rule our clime,
Nothing is sweeter to a death-filled mind,
Long in the grip of frosts, but than to find
Your pale gloom stretching infinite through time,
– Unless it be, one moonless night, we twain,
To reach some unsafe bed and numb our pain.'

Nathan Who's that by?

Pierre It's called 'Mists and Rains' . . . Guess.

Édith It's by you.

Pierre 'O ends of autumn, winters, mud-stained springs,/ Comatose seasons! . . . ' I'm very honoured, my dear, but it's by Monsieur Charles Baudelaire.

Nathan Tell me, Julienne, does he often bestow these little poems on you of an evening?

Julienne Sometimes. It happens. Except it's usually in the mornings!

Pierre In the morning, Victor Hugo! In the evening, Baudelaire or Apollinaire . . . You're going to miss your train, Élisa.

Nathan There's plenty of time, the train is at eight.

Alex *(to Élisa)* Why are you going back?

Élisa Because I don't want to spend the night here . . .

Alex Why?

Élisa Because . . .

Alex Because what?

Élisa Because I have to get back . . .

Alex Is someone waiting for you?

Élisa No . . .

Alex Well, then.

Slight pause.

Élisa *(smiling)* If I overdo it with the artichoke liqueur, I'll end up staying!

Alex Do you want to stay?

Élisa Listen, Alex, I've decided to leave, I'm taking the eight o'clock train and that's it!

Alex But I don't understand why you want to leave . . . Is it because of me?

Élisa No . . .

Alex *(to Pierre)* You could take her back tomorrow morning?

Pierre Of course!

Alex You can go back with them tomorrow morning, what's the problem?

Élisa I don't understand why you're insisting . . .

Alex Suppose I ask you to stay?

Élisa Why?

Alex You need a reason?

Édith For God's sake, let her do what she wants! Why flog it to death?

Élisa Thank you, Édith . . .

Alex I'm the one you should be thanking. Get that straight.

Pierre Why don't you let the girl make up her own mind? (*to Élisa*) Make your decision at the last minute, like a sensible person!

Élisa I second the motion . . .

Pierre You're very quiet, Nathan!

Nathan The discussion is closed, isn't it?

Pierre I didn't know your father was a writer. I'm completely changing the subject, but I never knew Simon wrote. It was a revelation to me this morning, when you read that piece . . .

Nathan He wrote when he was young . . . I don't think he persevered with it.

Pierre If ever there was a man . . .

Nathan You couldn't imagine being a writer . . .

Pierre Yes! It's almost a contradiction in terms . . . A mind as fundamentally abstract as his, inclined towards mathematics and music, it's impossible to imagine him giving himself over to literature!

Alex I fail to see the contradiction.

Pierre It's in the act itself . . . The physical commitment, the emotional commitment . . . Anyway, I know what

I mean! (*He leans over and pours some whisky into his glass.*) Oh, old age! We say such stupid things when we're old!

Julienne You don't think we ought to take a glance at the *pot-au-feu*, do you, Édith?

Édith Everything's fine. I checked it on the way back in.

Pierre (*to Alex*) That's why he was in such despair about you not becoming a writer . . .

Alex Well now, see, this was the conclusion I was waiting for as soon as you started and all the time I was hoping it wouldn't arrive.

Pierre Wrong again!

Alex Yes, wrong again.

Pierre I'm sorry! None of this matters at all. It's the monsoon out there.

Alex I have nothing to say. I never have had anything to say. How can you be a writer when, strictly speaking, you have nothing to say?

Pierre I don't believe you have nothing to say . . .

Alex Oh, you don't? . . . You think I do have something to say? What? Tell me, what, we'll save a lot of time.

Pierre You know what, old chap, I'm tired. I don't have the strength to bugger about.

Alex You tell me I have something to say. I'm asking you what? If you know better than I do?

Édith If you have nothing to say, why don't you shut up! I can't see why you're being such a pain in the arse!

Alex Pow! . . . Such language from sweet little Édith, I didn't know you could be like that . . .

Édith Well, now you know.

Alex Yes, now I know . . . Have you made a decision, Élisa? It's no use looking at Nathan. I'm sure he wants you to stay . . .

Édith If she's staying, we'll have to light the stove in the downstairs bedroom, it's running with damp.

Nathan No point. Honestly.

Pause.

If Élisa stays, she won't be using that bedroom.

Édith Then which one will she use?

Nathan Mine.

Édith And which one will you use?

Nathan Mine as well, what do you expect? To put it another way, we'll spend the night together . . . If Élisa stays!

Silence.

Édith I think I must be dreaming . . . (*to Élisa*) What are you going to do?! Say something!

Silence.

Well, say something! Everyone making decisions for you and you're stuck there like a slab of marble! Speak!

Nathan I can't see why you're getting in this state . . .

Édith I don't understand any of this! I feel like I'm living in a lunatic asylum! . . . On the day of Daddy's burial!

She's crying.

Nathan Exactly.

Édith What do you mean, exactly?

Nathan On the day of Daddy's burial . . .

Édith You're obliged to sleep with this whore?! . . .
Can't you say something, Élisa? I'm begging you, say
something! . . . Daddy . . . Daddy, come back! . . . I
want to die . . .

Julienne (*taking her in her arms*) Calm down, Édith,
calm down . . .

Élisa Alex, drive me to the station, please.

Alex You're wrong . . .

Élisa Please . . .

Nathan I'll drive you.

Élisa Let's go . . . (*She gets up.*)

Alex Wait! (*Silence.*) One minute? I have something to
say. Just one word . . . Well, perhaps a little more than
one word . . . (*Pause.*) On this day of mourning . . .
there was something missing . . . some event, some
speech . . . In this room, there was someone I believed
to be gone for good . . . who has just proved the
opposite . . . That's all. (*to Élisa*) Now you can do what
you like.

Élisa Are you sure that's all?

Alex She's crying . . . You're leaving . . . (*He turns to
Nathan and stares at him.*) I on the other hand have an
immense feeling of gratitude . . . That really is all. (*to
Pierre*) Any chance of a cigar?

    Pierre offers him the packet. Alex helps himself.

Édith Me too, please . . .

Alex See, there's something about these cigars . . .

He lights Édith's cigar and hands the packet back to Pierre. Pause.

Nathan (*to Élisa*) I'm still at your disposal . . .

Élisa We'll go. (*She moves towards Pierre, extending her hand.*) Goodbye . . .

Pierre Take an umbrella!

Élisa Yes . . . Goodbye, Julienne . . .

Julienne Goodbye, Élisa . . .

Élisa Did I have a coat?

Édith It's hanging in the hall cupboard . . .

Élisa leans forward, furtively kisses Édith and turns to leave.

Alex What about me, you're not going to say goodbye to me?

Élisa Goodbye . . .

Édith catches hold of Élisa's arm.

Édith Don't go . . .

Slight pause.

Alex Are we hoping to achieve a peak of ridiculousness? (*to Élisa*) Two false exits in one day, that's going it a bit, isn't it?

Édith Don't go, for pity's sake . . . I haven't the strength to speak . . .

Élisa Twice is a lot, Édith, he's right . . .

Pierre You haven't left the room yet . . .

Alex You sticking your oar in as well!

Pierre I'm not interfering. I'm making a comment . . .

Élisa (*to Alex*) Help me . . .

Alex That's what I've been doing . . . I've been watching you, you know, since this morning. I know everything about you, your gestures, your face, the way you move, the way you speak . . . I know exactly how you'll leave the room, how you'll close the door and pull on your coat . . . You won't say anything in the car, you'll light a cigarette . . . you'll pretend to be sad . . . And I don't care, I couldn't care less . . . I was expecting to be distraught, if I'd seen you again under any other circumstances, I would certainly have run after my illusions . . . Go on, bugger off!

Élisa recoils, she moves past Nathan and leaves. Nathan's getting ready to follow her, then he stops and turns back towards Alex. He's searching for what he wants to say . . . Finally, with a gesture of impotence, he smiles.

Nathan You've aged a lot today . . . You'd better watch yourself!

Alex smiles. Nathan leaves.
Silence.
Alex takes a few steps and sits down in Élisa's seat.

Alex No word from the philosopher?

Pierre Am I the philosopher?

Alex Pierrot the philosopher . . . (*to Édith*) Stop crying. Blow your nose, it's all over.

Édith I've ruined everything . . .

Alex You haven't . . .

Édith Yes, I have . . .

Alex You haven't!

Silence.

All right, Julienne?

Julienne Yes, yes . . .

Alex Families, not much fun, eh?

Julienne Listen, Alex, please, stop talking to me as if I was mentally defective . . .

Alex Well, all right!

Julienne It's extremely unpleasant, I assure you.

Alex You think they were right to leave?

Julienne What a question!

Alex There's no catch in it. I'd just be curious to hear your opinion.

Julienne I don't know, what is it you're expecting me to say?

Alex The Peugeot's at the end of the drive, they'll be soaked . . . Élisa'll be furious, her hair goes all frizzy when it rains . . . (*Pause.*) I feel good . . . I feel absolutely empty and good.

Silence.

Pierre Empty . . . Yes.

Alex Where did you two meet?

Pierre Oh, dear, oh, dear . . . Where was it?

Julienne sighs.

Through the personal columns.

Julienne Over my dead body . . .

Pierre Underneath the arcades in the Palais-Royal . . .

Julienne At a mutual friend's, boring as that.

Alex Was it love at first sight? . . .

Pierre For her, yes.

Julienne You know, you're really tiring.

Pause.

Pierre She was wearing a tam-o'-shanter . . .

Julienne A tam-o'-shanter!

Pierre What d'you call it? A cloak?

Julienne A cloak! A tam-o'-shanter's a hat, you buffoon.

Pierre All right, then, a cloak, and we were in fact walking underneath the arcades in the Palais-Royal, without my being able to take her arm for a single second, given the shape of the garment! . . .

Julienne You could easily have taken my arm, all I needed was to bring it out.

Pierre Ah, but you didn't . . .

Silence.

Alex Go on . . . I love these stories.

Pierre The memory's little delicacies . . .

Alex More . . . indulge me.

Julienne Little delicacies! . . . When he's on form, I say when he's on form, what I mean is when there's a big enough audience and they're paying attention, obviously, he's capable of making up the most terrible stories about us. I've heard him tell stories, not only with no beginning or end, but stories which, on top of everything else, finally make us look ridiculous.

Pierre You know what she does when that happens? She says, 'No! What are you talking about?' What's it look like?

Julienne Absolutely not. I never say anything.

Pierre You make a face . . . which is worse.

Julienne Not at all.

   Silence.

Alex More . . .

Pierre More?

Alex More . . .

Pierre Not a big enough audience, you know . . . (*He smiles.*) Shortage of spectators! (*to Édith, who has got up*) Where are you going?

Édith To the kitchen. (*She leaves.*)

Pierre (*to Julienne*) Perhaps you should go and help her . . . Don't leave her on her own . . .

   Julienne gets up.

Julienne Is your brother coming back? . . . What are we going to do with that great big *pot-au-feu* if there's only four of us?

Pierre We'll give it to the cats.

Julienne (*to Alex*) You have a cat?!

Pierre There must be stray cats, wandering about . . .

   Julienne leaves.

She can't bear the idea of waste. She's not particularly domestic, but the idea of waste, she's just like that . . . Are you in a dream?

Alex Am I in a dream? . . .

*Flowing water is heard and a regular clattering sound.
Alex is stretched out in the armchair, his eyes half
closed.*

Pierre What's making that noise?

Alex The gutter.

Pierre Ah . . .

Alex I tied it up with rags, practically killed myself.
Didn't you see it?

Pierre Yes, yes, I saw it.

Silence.

Is your sister still seeing the . . . I can't remember his
name, the wine merchant?

Alex Jean Santini. Yes.

Pierre Is he Corsican?

Alex Italian . . . By origin.

Pierre I had an accountant called Santini. He was
Corsican.

Alex Oh, yes . . .

Pierre Extremely Corsican . . . You're sure this fellow
isn't Corsican?

Alex Positive.

Pierre So, it's still going on . . . I didn't dare ask her
today, it seemed a bit . . . I must say, your gutter's in a
really bad way!

Alex I like it . . . I like the sound . . .

Pierre Yes . . . Well . . .

Silence.

Oh, it's so wonderful, being old . . . Sod it!

Silence.
Julienne returns.

Julienne (*to Pierre, under her breath*) She's crying . . .

Pierre (*after a pause*) Édith!

Alex Leave her alone . . . There's nothing you can do . . .

Julienne She wants to be alone . . . We have to leave her alone . . . Are there no other lights in here? Why don't you switch on this lamp? Is it working?

Alex Try it . . .

Julienne switches on the lamp.

Julienne That's better, isn't it?

Pierre Sit down.

Julienne I'm going to take the glasses out.

Pierre We'll do it later.

Julienne All right.

Pierre You have to keep moving, don't you?

Julienne No, no, I'm sitting down.

Pause.

What's that drumming sound?

Pierre The gutter.

Julienne The gutter's making that noise?

Pierre Yes.

Pause.

Julienne I picked up this shawl in the front hall, I can't say it goes very well . . . Don't you think it's cold? And I checked, the radiators are on.

Pierre It's the damp.

Julienne Definitely. The walls are damp.

Édith arrives, very distressed.

Édith There's someone at the door . . . Someone's trying to get in! Can you hear?!

Slight pause. Nathan and Élisa come into the room.

Nathan It's us . . . (*Pause. To Élisa*) Come on.

He takes her by the arm. They both approach.

We saw a shadow flitting past in the corridor. Was that you?

Édith I heard the lock . . . I thought someone was forcing the door . . .

Nathan It wasn't locked, we just opened it.

Édith I heard a noise.

Slight pause.

Pierre You came back . . . or you never left?

Nathan We left . . . and we came back. (*to Élisa*) Sit down.

Élisa sits down nervously.
Silence.

Julienne She's frozen stiff, poor little thing! (*She gets up and hands Élisa the shawl.*) Here, wrap yourself up in this . . . I'm sorry, Édith, I found it in the front hall, I imagine it must be yours.

Édith (*to Élisa*) Are you cold? Do you need a sweater? I've plenty of things upstairs.

Élisa No, no, not at all. Thanks. This'll do fine.

She puts the shawl around her shoulders and smiles at Édith. Édith smiles back.

It smells good when you come back . . .

Édith Does it?

Élisa Oh, yes. Very good.

Pause.
Élisa looks at Alex.

Two false exits.

Alex In one day . . . Why not?

Silence.

Pierre So you really did leave and come back? (*to Julienne*) What? I'm not asking a question! . . . My wife's very disapproving, but I'm not asking any questions!

Nathan We left this house . . . Yes . . . Édith? . . . Come closer . . . What are you doing over there? . . . We walked across the garden in the rain . . . We got in the car . . . I switched on the engine . . . I turned on the windscreen wipers . . . and the lights . . . Élisa said nothing . . . She didn't light a cigarette, she didn't even pretend to be sad . . . We stayed where we were for perhaps a minute? . . . During the minute, something strange and sudden occurred . . . Gien Station, which we imagine to be in Gien, was there, at the end of the drive . . . the clock on the facade showed seven o'clock, we had an hour to kill . . .

Pause.
He paces up and down, Crosses to the window . . .
Then he turns back.

There were all kinds of people on the forecourt, shadows with luggage, silhouettes of drivers, taxis, hotel lights,

sounds of streetcars braking in puddles . . . I said to
Élisa, 'Let's go to a café . . . ' I don't remember what
we ordered . . . I told her something I'd remembered
from this very station about thirty years ago, and she
said to me, 'I loathe stations' . . . We agreed this sensation
of not being anywhere had to do with evening and the
provinces . . . And while we were talking, the hands
on the clock turned and the hour trickled away . . .
We crossed the road, we rushed to the booking office
to buy the ticket . . . then the platform, the whistle,
the first carriage where she got on . . . There was the
slamming of doors, that grinding of iron and the train
was gone . . . I watched it disappear into the countryside,
and she, from her window, watched the countryside
melt away . . . And the station disappeared as well . . .
I switched off the engine, turned out the lights and we
set off back the way we came, running as fast as we
could . . .

Silence.

Alex (*to Pierre*) Now do you know why I never became
a writer? . . . Precisely because of this . . . This sort of
thing . . . When I get to this point, the page has always
stayed blank . . . (*to Élisa*) You left . . . We stayed here,
all four of us, sitting here, within these four walls, me
here, in this same spot, I didn't move . . . And then,
another strange thing happened, very strange . . . I was
sitting in the Peugeot, in the back, you were in front,
Nathan was driving, he'd turned on the windscreen
wipers double-speed, I remember this particularly, the
rubber's perished, they make a scraping noise . . . we
went through Dampierre and you put on a cassette . . .
you put on a cassette and it was a Schubert quintet . . .
You turned round and asked me if it was too loud and
I said, 'No, no, no, no . . . don't change anything,

whatever you do, don't change a thing.' You didn't
change anything and I tipped back my head and watched
the trees, the flowing lights, the drops of water bursting
against the windows, Nathan's expression in the rear-
view mirror, Nathan's contented expression, and the
night . . . The fog and the night . . . And I was, how can
I put it, emptied, weightless in the back seat, trusting,
protected, a sense of indescribable well-being . . .

   Pause.

. . . That's exactly what writing is, going somewhere
you're not going . . . And already there, no matter what
you do, already there on the blank page, is the return,
the end of the adventure . . . When I was twenty, I used
to imagine my complete works, seven volumes on India
paper, a world of giants, tempestuous, borne aloft by
the swell, a prey to God knows what kind of frenzy . . .
Tumultuous beings, beings capable of ingesting the
world, all-inclusive, full of genius and strength and
exhaustion . . . That's how coruscating I was when I was
twenty . . . And instead of all that, came the everyday
fixtures and fittings, the small wound at the centre of
the world, the interminable flow of desires and journeys
and useless gestures . . . The labyrinth of useless
pathways . . . Not to mention sensitivity . . . paralysing
sensitivity . . . (*Pause.*) And the superlative *pot-au-feu*
which Édith has prepared for us and which I intend to
sprinkle with every living spice in the kitchen!

Édith Just try it!

Alex You'll see!

   Silence.

Édith I telephoned Jean just now. He's on his way.

Alex Mr Tsetse Fly is coming to dinner?

Édith Mr Tsetse Fly is coming to spend the night . . .
He won't get here till midnight.

Pierre 'One moonless night, we twain . . . '

Julienne Stop it, Pierre. Shut up, just this once.

Pause.

Alex Let's go and eat!

Élisa Already?

Alex You mean at last!

Blackout.

LIFE x 3

Life × 3 in this translation was first presented in the Lyttelton auditorium of the Royal National Theatre, London, on 7 December 2000. The cast, in order of speaking, was as follows:

Henry Mark Rylance
Sonia Harriet Walter
Inez Imelda Staunton
Hubert Oliver Cotton

Musician Walter Fabeck (keyboards)

Director Matthew Warchus
Designer Mark Thompson
Lighting Designer Hugh Vanstone
Music Gary Yershon
Sound Designer Christopher Shutt
Company Voice Work Patsy Rodenburg

Yasmina Reza and Christopher Hampton would like to thank Catherine McMillan for her contribution to the translation

Note

At the author's wish, the text that follows
is that of the American version of the play, as revised
with Christopher Hampton. The text of the version
as performed in London was published by
Faber and Faber in a single volume in 2000.

Characters

Henry
Sonia
Inez
Hubert

Voice of
The Child

One

Evening
   A living room. As abstract as possible. No walls, no doors; as if open to the sky. What's important is the suggestion of a living room.
   Sonia is sitting down, wearing a bathrobe. She's looking through a file. Henry appears.

Henry He wants a cookie.

Sonia He just brushed his teeth.

Henry He's asking for a cookie.

Sonia He knows very well there's no cookies in bed.

Henry You tell him.

Sonia Why didn't you?

Henry Because I didn't know there were no cookies in bed.

Sonia How could you not know there were no cookies in bed? Cookies have never been allowed in bed, nothing sweet is.

   She goes out.
   Pause.
   The child starts crying. She comes back.

Henry What's the matter with him?

Sonia He wants a cookie.

Henry Why is he crying?

Sonia Because I said no. He's becoming disgustingly temperamental.

Slight pause.

Henry Give a him a slice of apple.

Sonia He doesn't want a slice of apple, he wants a cookie, and in any case he's not getting anything. You don't eat in bed, you eat at the table, you don't eat in bed after you've brushed your teeth, and now I need to look through this file, I have a ten o'clock meeting in the morning.

The child continues crying.
Henry goes out. The child stops crying.
Henry comes back.

Henry He's agreed to a slice of apple.

Sonia He's not having any apple, he's not having anything, you don't eat in bed, the subject is closed.

Henry You tell him.

Sonia Stop it.

Henry I said yes to the apple, I thought the apple was a possibility. If you're saying no, go and tell him yourself.

Pause.

Sonia Take him in a slice of apple and tell him you're doing it behind my back. Tell him I said no and that you're only doing it because you said yes, but that I can't find out because I'm radically opposed to any kind of food in bed.

Henry Should I peel it?

Sonia Yes.

Henry goes out.

Pause. He comes back

Henry He wants you to give him a hug.

Sonia I've already given him a hug.

Henry Go and give him a little hug.

Sonia How many more times are we supposed to go back in his room?

Henry Just a little hug. I calmed him down, he'll go to sleep.

Sonia goes out. Pause.
  The child starts crying. She comes back.
  She sits down in silence. She picks up her file.

Now what's the matter with him?

Sonia He wants the whole apple.

Pause.
  They go back to what they were doing.

Henry Why don't we give him the whole apple? It's good that he likes fruit.

Sonia He's not having any more.

Henry If you like, I'll peel it and take it in to him.

Sonia Spoil him. What do I care? Do what you like.

Henry (*towards the child*) Arnaud, night-night!

Sonia He's a pain in the ass.

Henry Night night!

Sonia The more you keep yelling 'night-night', the more worked up he gets.

Henry We're not spending the rest of the evening listening to him snivel. I don't understand why you're being so inflexible. What difference is a little apple going to make to the course of history?

Sonia If we give in on the apple, he'll know he can get us to give in on anything.

Henry All you have to do is tell him we're giving in on the apple this evening and this evening only, to be nice to him and because we're tired of listening to him whining.

Sonia Definitely not because we're tired of listening to him whining!

Henry Yes, right, that's what I meant, from now on we're never going to give in again, especially if he whines at the least little setback, because that's only going to stiffen our resolve.

Sonia To say we're tired of listening to him whining is the worst possible way of expressing it. It's inconceivable that you could even come up with an expression like that.

Henry We're *tired*, in the general sense of the word, of listening to him whining. Generally speaking, we're up to *here* with the sound of whining.

Sonia Hence the whole apple.

Henry Hence the apple, hence the final, exceptional apple.

> *Sonia reads.*
> *Henry goes out.*
> *Very soon, the child stops snivelling. Henry comes back.*

He was pleased. In fact, you know, I think he really was hungry. I explained to him it was imperative he improve his behaviour. Imperative. He wants a hug. Just a little hug.

Sonia No.

Henry A little hug.

Sonia (*parodying him*) . . . a little hug.

Henry I told him you were coming.

  Sonia gets up.

(*towards the child*) Mommy's coming!

  Sonia goes out.
    Henry's on his own.
    Quite soon, the child starts crying.
    Sonia comes back.

Sonia I'm not going in there one more time, I hope that's clear.

Henry What's happening? Every time you go in there, he cries.

Sonia What's that supposed to mean?

Henry I don't know. Every time you go into his room, he starts crying again.

Sonia So?

Henry When I go in, he calms down and gets ready to go to sleep like a good boy.

Sonia And when I go in, he screams his head off.

Henry What did you say to him?

Sonia To make him scream his head off?

Henry Listen, you have to admit it's strange, it's as if you upset him every time you go in.

Sonia You know what he wanted? He didn't want 'a little hug', he wanted a story. He wanted to hear a fourth story while he was scarfing his apple.

Henry Arnaud, night-night!

Sonia Shut up, Arnaud!

Henry Don't talk to him like that.

Sonia Shut the fuck up, Arnaud!

   The child stops crying.

Henry Are you out of your mind?

Sonia He's stopped. There you are.

Henry He's stopped because he's traumatised.

Sonia You couldn't traumatise anyone, that's for sure. Not your son and not Hubert Finidori.

Henry What's Hubert Finidori got to do with it?

Sonia I'd like to record you when you're on the phone with him. Your kowtowing, your obsequious tone of voice.

The Child (*from its room*) Daddy!

Henry Yes, darling! (*on his way out*) Perhaps you'll explain to me what Hubert Finidori is doing in this conversation.

   Sonia's started reading again.
   Henry comes back.

He's very upset.

   No reaction from her.

He can't understand how a mother could be so violent.

Sonia Poor little pumpkin.

Henry Sonia, if you carry on like this and that boy goes on being a pain in the ass, I'm going.

Sonia Go.

Henry I'm going and I'm not coming back.

Sonia Who's stopping you?

Henry wrenches the file out of Sonia's hands and throws it on the floor.

Henry Go and give him a kiss, go and tell him you're sorry you lost all sense of proportion.

Sonia Let go of me!

Henry I won't let you go until you've apologised.

Sonia Apologised for what? You couldn't take my side just for once in your life! Apologised for what? For not having taken him in a box of chocolate fingers? Do you want a box of chocolate fingers, Arnaud?

Henry You're hysterical!

Sonia Here's a box of chocolate fingers, Arnaud, you want it?

Henry Stop it!

Sonia Daddy's bringing you a box of chocolate fingers!

Henry is trying to put his hand over her mouth.

The Child (*from its room*) Daddy!

Henry That's enough, Arnaud!

They grapple.

Sonia Why are you telling him that's enough, poor thing, we offered him the chocolate fingers!

Henry Be quiet!

Sonia You're suffocating me!

Henry He can hear everything!

Sonia Help!

We leave them with brutal abruptness, in mid-action.

*

Evening The street.

Inez I have a run in my hose!

Hubert It doesn't show.

Inez Because it just started. It can only get worse.

Hubert It really doesn't matter.

Inez Hubert, I am not going to visit people I've never met before with a run in my hose.

Hubert We're already a half-hour late, we can't go back home, and we can't go shopping for pantyhose in the middle of the night. Let's just rise above it.

Inez You rushed me and this is what happens. Is it far? Why did you park so far away? There are dozens of spaces, look, who'd want to live here?

Hubert Haven't you got any nail polish?

Inez Nail polish?

Hubert To stop the run?

Inez And look like some bag lady?

Hubert It's nine-twenty.

Inez I cannot show up with a run in my pantyhose!

Hubert Who's going to notice?

Inez Who's going to notice? Everyone, except for you, if someone shows up at my house with a run in her pantyhose, the run's the first thing I notice.

Hubert All you do is tell Henry's wife you snagged your pantyhose in the elevator, that you're very embarrassed, and if you're lucky she'll lend you a pair. Inez, we don't give a shit about these people, he hasn't published in three years, he needs my support to be made Research Director, who cares if there's a run in your pantyhose, they'll be licking our boots.

*

Back at Sonia and Henry's.
  They come out of the child's room together.

Henry You've terrified him.

Sonia Henry, we discussed all this, let's not start again.

Henry A six-year-old child, hearing his mother screaming for help. Think about it.

Sonia We calmed him down, the subject is closed.

Henry In his own home! In his own home! Which means the aggressor can only be me. His father.

Sonia Arnaud accepted that we were joking.

Henry To humour us. He's much sharper than you think.

Sonia The subject is closed.

  She plunges back into her files.

Henry So. I'm obsequious when I talk to Hubert Finidori?

The door buzzer sounds.

Sonia (*under her breath*) Who's that?

Henry (*under his breath*) I'll go look.

He comes back immediately.
All the following exchanges under their breath.

The Finidoris!

Sonia It's tomorrow!

Henry It's the seventeenth . . . it's tonight.

Sonia This is a catastrophe!

Henry Yes.

Sonia Did they hear us?

Henry Why, what did we say?

Sonia We can't let them in.

Henry We can't not let them in.

Sonia What are we going to do?

Henry Go and . . . go and fix yourself up a bit.

Sonia Are we going to let them in?

Henry They know we're here.

Sonia This is a catastrophe.

Henry Is there anything left in the kitchen?

Sonia We cleaned it out. I thought it was tomorrow.

Henry This was a very important dinner for me!

Sonia You're saying it's my fault!

Henry At least go and change.

Sonia No.

Henry You cannot receive the Finidoris in your
bathrobe!

Sonia Yes, I can.

*Henry pushes her towards the back of the apartment,
trying not to make any noise.*

Henry Will you go and get dressed, Sonia?

Sonia (*resisting his pressure*) No.

They struggle in silence. The buzzer sounds again.

Henry How can you be so selfish?

The buzzer sounds again.

I'm letting them in.

*

Inez, Hubert, Sonia and Henry in the living room.
*The two guests are picking at various snacks
('Laughing Cow' cheese, a box of chocolate fingers, etc.)
set out on a tray. They have drinks, as do Sonia and
Henry.*
*Sonia has changed. Inez still has a run in her
pantyhose.*

Inez Me too, I'm very much on top of the rituals of
bedtime. First of all, the time, we go to bed at eight
o'clock, well, that is, we can stretch it to eight-thirty, but
anyway, let's say between eight and eight-thirty, whatever
happens, by eight-thirty we are in bed, with ultra-clean
teeth, because, to be honest, in the morning, I find it
difficult to make them brush their teeth before school,
I know it's wrong, in fact teeth ought to be brushed, at
the very least, in the morning and at night, but oh well,

I turn a blind eye in the morning, whereas at night, they know this is something fundamental and that obviously eating anything at all afterwards is out of the question. As for Hubert, it's strange, he agrees with the parenting guidelines, but on the other hand he'll go and get them all worked up by starting a game of soccer with them, in their room, at eight o'clock at night.

Everyone laughs.

Hubert Once. Once, I played soccer.

Inez Once you played soccer, but you regularly get them all worked up.

Henry So you're very strict on teeth.

Inez Oh, yes. Yes, very strict on teeth. Basically, it's not so much teeth as discipline. Although I'm very much on top of the hygienic aspect, of course, but teeth is discipline. You go to bed, you brush your teeth.

Sonia (*to Henry*) You see!

Henry Arnaud brushes his teeth.

Sonia And then afterwards you peel him an apple.

Inez (*laughing pleasantly*) Oh, no. No! If you peel him an apple after his teeth, the whole system collapses.

Henry When I wash my hands, it's very rare for me not to touch anything afterwards.

Hubert Well done, Henry. Their theories will kill us. What we need is women you can switch off once in a while. They're not so bad, these little cookies. (*He munches a chocolate finger.*) So, how far have you gotten with the flatness of halos?

Henry I've finished. I'm submitting the paper before the end of the month.

Hubert Excellent. Having said that, you ought to check on Astro PH, I have the impression a similar piece has been submitted to the *AP-J*.

The Child (*from its room*) Mommy!

Henry (*shattered*) Oh, yes? Is this very recent?

Hubert Yes, yes, this morning, a Mexican team: 'On the Flatness of Galaxy Halos.'

The Child Mommy!

Henry 'On the Flatness of Galaxy Halos'? That's my subject! What's he want? Sonia, go take a look, darling!

Sonia goes out.

You've got me worried, Hubert.

Hubert Check before you get upset about it.

Henry I left my laptop at the Institute.

The child starts crying.

Henry What's wrong with him tonight! 'On the Flatness of Galaxy Halos' is my subject! 'Are the Dark Matter Halos of Galaxies Flat?' What's the difference?

Hubert Perhaps they're dealing with visible matter. I just skimmed over the abstract. (*He munches the last chocolate finger.*) Although I've got to say it troubled me, that's why I'm bringing it up.

The child's crying is still audible.

Inez Maybe he should read it before he starts worrying.

Hubert Inez, my love, don't interrupt when you don't know what you're talking about.

Henry (*loudly*) What's the matter with him, Sonia!

Inez Why depress him in advance?

Sonia comes back.

Sonia He wants chocolate fingers.

Henry This is insane.

Sonia He's had his apple, now he wants chocolate fingers.

Hubert (*flourishing the empty box*) I hope he doesn't mean these delicious things I've just been eating.

Sonia He does.

Henry And a good thing too! We're not giving him chocolate fingers in bed at ten o'clock at night.

Hubert I'm appalled. Was this the last box?

Inez No, listen, Hubert, they're not going to give him chocolate fingers in bed at ten o'clock at night!

Henry Of course we're not.

Sonia We could give him some cheese.

Henry Sonia, what's got into you?

Sonia You'd rather he ruined the evening? At least we'll have some peace.

Inez That's what he's counting on.

Sonia I'm sorry?

Inez He's making himself obnoxious so that you'll give in.

Sonia And we are giving in.

Inez And you're wrong.

Hubert Look, Inez, don't interfere . . .

Inez I'll interfere any way I like, stop trying to muzzle me!

Henry (*to Sonia*) Take him some cheese, take him whatever you like as long as he stops interrupting us! What was their approach? Theoretical models or numerical simulations?

Hubert I think models, but as I said . . .

Henry (*interrupting him*) Theoretical models! I'm fucked. Two years' work blown to fuck.

   The child has stopped crying.

Hubert Don't go off the deep end, Henry! I say models but maybe it's simulations, and in any case maybe they've only modelled the visible matter!

Inez What's your subject in layman's terms?

Henry Are the dark matter halos of galaxies flat?

Inez And are they flat, do you think?

Henry I think they're ten times as thin as they're wide.

Inez Right . . .

   Sonia comes back.

Sonia He doesn't want cheese, he doesn't want anything, he wants chocolate fingers and you absolutely shouldn't feel bad about having finished the box, because we wouldn't have given him any.

Henry What's he doing?

Sonia Crying. I closed all the doors so we wouldn't hear him.

Inez Poor little pumpkin.

Sonia Did you get enough to eat? I'm so embarrassed.

Henry If it hadn't been for Arnaud, we could have taken you out to dinner.

Hubert Henry, stop looking so lugubrious. Even if your approaches are similar, which is by no means established, you'll undoubtedly have reached different conclusions.

Inez Of course you will!

Hubert See, and she knows what she's talking about!

Inez No one's laughing. Least of all poor Henry.

Hubert I know how to make Henry laugh! Henry, you feel like a laugh, ask Inez to describe a halo for you.

Sonia Henry has his own in-house ignoramus.

Inez I'm not offended, you know!

Henry That paper is my scientific death warrant. It's worrying me, not being able to hear him. Open the doors, Sonia, please, I have enough to worry about for one evening!

Inez What do you think's going to happen?

Henry Nothing. But when my son is crying, I prefer to hear it.

Sonia You maybe, but not necessarily our guests.

Inez Open the doors, don't worry about us.

Hubert Don't worry about us.

Sonia goes back towards the child's room.

Anyway, my friend, you seem a little sensitive this evening. Scientific death warrant!

Sonia comes back. The child is not to be heard.

Henry Three years without publishing, only to see your subject refused because it's already been covered, what do you call that? A scientific death warrant.

Hubert We're not in America!

Henry It's worse here in France. At least over there you know where you stand. I can't hear him, has he calmed down?

Sonia So it seems.

Henry You didn't go in to see him?

Sonia No.

Henry It's not normal for him to stop crying suddenly just like that.

Inez You mollycoddle him, Henry.

Hubert She's terrible! (*to Inez*) You are terrible.

Henry Now I'm going to have to start again, to take their work into account. I'm going to have to quote them, I'm going to have to quote them, and who's probably going to be asked to referee my paper? Them.

Hubert So what? In six months you'll be telling me they've prepared the best referee's report you've ever had. You must be at the end of your rope, or why make such a drama out of it?

Inez (*to Hubert*) And what possible reason could you have for telling him about this paper?

Henry Thank God! Thank God he did tell me about it! Thank you, Hubert. Sincerely, thank you.

Sonia For what? For ruining your weekend?

Henry Thank you for tipping me off. Thank you for stopping me from looking like a fool on Monday morning at the office. I'm sure by now Raoul Arestegui, who lives in front of his screen, has already made a dozen phone calls.

Hubert Frankly, I thought I had to tell you, but I didn't expect this leap into the irrational.

Sonia You could have put it another way.

Hubert Could I? (*He gropes around inside a packet of pistachios, but it's empty.*)

Henry (*with alacrity*) Are there none left? Sonia, you could bring out those little crackers, would you like something salty, something salty or something sweet? What do we have left, darling?

Hubert No, no, don't worry about it.

Sonia You could have warned him some other way, used words which would just leave some vague, inconspicuous scent in the air.

Hubert My dear Sonia, we're in the realm of science. Words are not aromatherapy. Unfortunately.

> *He's amused himself with this sally and turns to Henry for approval. Henry laughs feebly.*

Sonia Whatever realm you claim to inhabit, the words you chose have plunged my husband into disarray.

Hubert It's the facts which have plunged him into disarray. And the disarray is entirely out of proportion.

Sonia The facts as you presented them. To trigger his disarray.

Henry You're insane. Come on, Sonia, this is ridiculous.

Hubert (*attempting to preserve a good-natured tone*) I wouldn't like to go up against her in court!

Sonia I haven't been in court for years, I work for a finance company.

Hubert But you still know how to use words which. . . how did it go . . .?

Henry Sonia, our friends are still hungry.

Sonia You want some Cheez-Its?

Inez No, thanks.

Hubert Ah, yes, Cheez-Its, I love Cheez-Its.

   Sonia goes out.

Henry Something stronger?

Hubert No, thanks, I'll stick with the Sancerre.

Inez Is it important for halos to be flat?

Hubert Feminine logic! She jumps all over me for mentioning it and now she brings up the subject again.

   Sonia has returned.

White Cheddar Cheez-Its! My favourite!

Inez Is it important?

Henry When you look at the Milky Way, does it seem to form a band? . . .

Inez Yes.

The Child Mommy!

Sonia Night night, Arnaud!

Henry Well, I have serious reasons to suppose that the distribution of dark matter which surrounds it is more or less as flat as the visible matter.

The Child Mommy! I'm thirsty!

Henry He's thirsty.

Inez What difference does that make?

Henry All the difference in the world. Until today the halo was assumed to be round. It was spherical! (*to Sonia*) You wouldn't like to take him in a little glass of water?

Sonia No.

Inez And what difference does it make if the halo's not round any more?

Henry To our everyday life, none.

Hubert Inez, stop bugging him with your inept questions.

The Child Mommy!

Henry It's a modification of a presumed reality. A new entry in the encyclopedia of mankind. Sonia, sweetheart, bring him a drink, we can't let him monopolise the evening!

Inez How old is he?

Sonia Six.

Inez Can't he get his own drink?

Sonia No.

Henry Yes, he can, of course he can, it's just that we don't like him to get out of bed.

Sonia He does not know how to get his own drink.

Henry He absolutely knows how to, but he's not allowed to get out of bed.

Sonia Arnaud does not know how to get his own drink.

Henry Of course he does!

Inez A six-year-old knows how to get his own drink.

Sonia Not our son.

Henry Arnaud knows perfectly well how to get his own drink, come on, Sonia!

Hubert If you ask me he knows how to, but he prefers to be served.

Henry Exactly!

Hubert He's a sultan!

Sonia goes out.

I haven't upset her, have I?

Henry Of course not.

Inez You're wrong to give in to all his whims.

Hubert Meddling again, Inez.

Inez What do you mean, meddling! Who called him a sultan?

Hubert I called him a sultan as a joke. I'm not telling people what to do.

Henry Two years' work blown to fuck . . .

Hubert Henry, for God's sake!

Henry Three years without publishing, even as a minor collaborator. In America people like that get bounced into teaching.

Sonia returns and heads towards the tray. She's looking for something.

Sonia Are there any more Cbeez-Its?

Henry Who for, for Arnaud?

Sonia He's had his glass of water and he promises not to bother us any more if he can have a bowl of Cheez-Its.

Hubert (*searching*) Don't tell me I've finished the Cheez-Its!

Henry (*finding one*) Here's one! One left.

Hubert Two!

Henry Two Cheez-Its, that should do, shouldn't it?

Sonia sets off again with the Cheez-Its.

Inez (*to Henry*) So you thought it was all your idea?

Hubert What idea, sweetheart?

Inez Hubert, please, stop trying to police everything I say!

Hubert I'm not trying to police everything you say, sweetheart, I just didn't understand your question . . .

Inez You understood it perfectly well, not that I was talking to you, but you understood it perfectly well, and this permanently ironic tone you use in response to everything I say as if I were an idiot is unbearable.

The child starts crying.

Hubert Now you've made him cry.

Henry What's going on, Sonia? Shit!

Hubert Calm down, let's all calm down, keep a sense of proportion.

Sonia comes back The child can no longer be heard.

Sonia Two Cheez-Its weren't enough, he's had a spanking, I don't want to talk about it.

Henry Have you closed the doors?

Sonia Yes.

Slight pause.

Hubert Have you been here long?

Sonia A year and a half.

Hubert Where were you before?

Sonia Montparnasse.

Hubert This is better. Quieter.

Sonia Yes.

Hubert And you no longer practise as a lawyer?

Sonia No.

Hubert Henry told me you were a lawyer, I imagined you practised as a lawyer.

Sonia I used to practise as a lawyer.

Hubert I see.

Henry A brilliant woman married to a failure.

Hubert Let's pretend we didn't hear that.

Sonia And you, Inez, what do you do?

Inez Nothing. That is, hundreds of things, I've never been as busy as I have since I stopped working.

Hubert That's why I never ask her for anything. Never ask a favour from someone who does nothing. They won't have the time. (*He amuses himself with this sally.*)

Inez My husband can only amuse himself at my expense. I can't imagine how he'd function socially if it wasn't for me. (*to Henry*) You haven't answered my question.

Henry Which was?

Hubert Is intergalactic plasma multiphased?

He laughs heartily at his own roguishness.
Sonia laughs involuntarily. Henry joins in late. Inez
is stone-faced.

Henry (*as the laughter of the other two continues*) You
were asking me if other people had tackled my subject.

Inez Thank you, Henry.

Henry I thought I was the first to set about trying to
solve it. Even if the question was topical.

Inez You told me your discovery was of no use to our
everyday life.

Hubert Topical means in the air, my love, in the spirit of
the age. Oh, look, there's one more Cheez-It!

Sonia Eat it.

Hubert You're kidding. I'm in enough trouble with the
boy as it is. Having said that, when we start to travel
among the galaxies in a thousand years' time, we'll have
to take account of Henry's calculations.

Henry Or those of my rival.

The Child (*in a desperate howl*) Daadeee! Daadeeee!

Henry For God's sake, I've had enough, I'm going to
bash his head in! Excuse me, two minutes . . . (*He starts
to leave.*)

Sonia I'm coming with you.

Hubert Give him the Cheez-It, give him the Cheez-It!

Ridiculously, Henry comes back to get the Cheez-Its.
They go out.
Inez and Hubert are on their own. They speak
under their breath.

Hubert They're insane.

Inez Especially him.

Hubert And the child is horrendous.

Inez He has no guidelines, they give him cheese at ten o'clock at night.

Hubert And we've been fed crap.

Inez Why do you put me down in front of other people? I wish I could understand this pathological need you have to continually put me down in front of other people.

Hubert I don't put you down. I was kidding.

Inez 'Ask Inez to describe a halo for you' – you think that's hilarious?

Hubert I was just trying to lighten the atmosphere, you saw the state he was in.

Inez Whose fault is that?

Hubert Inez, I'm not going to put up with this catalogue . . .

Inez Sh! . . .

Hubert (*resumes in a muffled and therefore even more exasperated voice*) . . . this catalogue of grievances every time we go out somewhere . . .

Inez Did you have to tell him about that paper?

Hubert Now you're shouting.

Inez That man's clinically depressed.

Hubert I'm not surprised.

Inez What do you mean?

Hubert In a competitive system, it's not having good ideas that counts, it's winning the race. He can kiss his promotion goodbye.

Henry (*offstage*) One more word, one more squeak and I'll carry out my threat!

Inez How can you be so cold?

Hubert I'm not cold, he's doomed. There are people who are doomed, it's sad but there's nothing you can do about it. You know it's really unbearable, that run in your pantyhose, it's been driving me nuts ever since we arrived.

Inez lashes out at him, a despairing blow.

Inez Who made me come up like this? I knew it looked awful.

Sonia comes back.

Sonia Who's doomed? My husband?

Hubert Henry? Doomed? Are you kidding? He's the only one who thinks he's doomed! We were talking about our friend Serge Bloch, who, after being flooded out . . .

Inez (*interrupting him*) We were talking about Henry.

Hubert (*cheerily*) There's a real wind of madness blowing through this place tonight! She hates me because I've just pointed out she has a run in her pantyhose.

Inez (*extremely animated*) You have not just pointed it out, my pantyhose got a run in the street and I didn't want to meet your friends looking like a gypsy. I was terribly embarrassed arriving at your apartment like this, I was getting ready to apologise and ask you to lend me a pair of hose, but since you were embarrassed yourself to have us show up tonight instead of tomorrow, I opted to behave as if nothing was wrong, an aristocratic stance which cost me blood, because – of course there's no reason you should know this, but I'm a rather particular woman, and my husband, instead of supporting me in this course of action, instead of protecting my dignity, can find nothing better to do than attack me in the middle of a conversation by saying the run in my panty-hose is unbearable and that I've ruined his evening . . .

Hubert I'm afraid Inez may have slightly overdone it with the Sancerre!

Inez Don't demean yourself by pretending I'm a lush, Hubert, your usual catty remarks will be more than enough . . .

Sonia I only have black pantyhose, I don't have any flesh-coloured, I don't know if they would do . . .

Inez Everything's fine. Don't worry about me. In any case I'm very happy to go on wearing something which is ruining my husband's evening . . .

Henry (*on his way back*) The slightest squeak, the slightest disturbance, and you can say goodbye to your kiddy-cassette!

Hubert Well done!

Henry It's been a rather disjointed evening, hasn't it? I am sorry.

Sonia (*to Inez*) You know, it doesn't matter at all, to tell you the truth I was going to answer the door in my bathrobe, Henry begged me to get changed, said I couldn't receive the Finidoris in my bathrobe.

Hubert Such a stickler for formalities, Henry!

Sonia Only when it's you, normally my husband couldn't give a shit about formalities, except when it's you. But when it's Hubert Finidori, my husband adopts a Finidorian tone, bows down and wants people to get changed.

Henry What do you mean, I bow down, what do you mean, a Finidorian tone, what are you talking about? What are you talking about, Sonia?!

Hubert And why do I deserve this special treatment? Please note I'm pretending not to notice the bile sloshing around behind all this.

Sonia The special treatment is because my husband imagines you're capable of having him promoted to Grade A.

Hubert Grade A! She knows what she's talking about, then, she's mastered the jargon.

Inez Hubert!

Henry Sonia, I'm appalled!

Hubert Henry is Research Scientist at the IAP and I'm lab-director at Meudon, in what way could I be responsible for his recruitment?

Sonia You're a member of the National Committee, you can approve the promotion of people who don't work in your lab.

Henry Hubert, I don't know what's eating at her, this is all ridiculous. I'm incredibly sorry.

Sonia An example of the Finidorian tone.

Henry Sonia!

Sonia It's obvious you're never going to do anything for my husband, you're enjoying seeing him squirm, you warned him about the paper by this competitor with the sole aim of watching him flounder and absolving yourself of all responsibility if he ever dared to come to you crawling for a favour. I find your perversity disgusting and I despise your pathetic string-pulling.

Inez My husband has been published in *Nature*, I fail to see what's pathetic about that.

Hubert Inez, Inez, I don't need your help, darling.

Henry Hubert is one of the greatest cosmological authorities in the world, there isn't a single paper on galaxy clusters which fails to mention him, so what do you know about it, Sonia? What are you talking about?

Sonia He just said you were doomed.

Hubert She's lethal! I can see why you tend to be a little erratic, Henry.

Henry What do you mean, doomed? Me, doomed?

Sonia That's what he just said. That you were doomed and there was nothing anybody could do for you.

Henry Who to? To you?

Sonia To her.

Inez Hubert was talking about Serge Bloch, you were talking about Serge Bloch, weren't you, Hubert? . . .

Henry What does Serge Bloch have to do with this?

Inez Well, first he was flooded out . . .

Hubert (*interrupting her*) Please, Inez, let's not make ourselves completely idiotic! First of all, Sonia, let me tell you that you'd have done better to receive us in your bathrobe. For one thing, it would have put the finishing touch to the incongruities of the occasion, but above all it would have made you more human. There's something dry and brittle about you, which is in total contrast to the pretty and flirtatious woman you first appear to be.

Henry Couldn't agree more!

Sonia I'd have done better to receive them in my bathrobe?

Inez You'd have done better not to receive us at all! This is the worst evening I've ever spent! (*She shows signs of preparing to leave.*)

Henry Congratulations, Sonia! Well done!

Hubert It's not her fault this evening's been a catastrophe, we've all played our part. Inez, angel, calm down.

Inez Don't call me angel and stop being so smarmy.

Henry Hubert, be honest, am I doomed?

Hubert You're going through a rough patch.

Henry In other words, I'm doomed.

Hubert You're not doomed, you're abnormally anxious and you're completely defeatist. Henry, maybe you should get some help.

Henry Did you really say I was doomed?

Hubert Of course not!

Henry And do you think I still have a chance of being published?

Hubert Certainly! Perhaps not in the *AP-J*, but in *A.&A.* Or in *Monthly Notices*, I don't see why not.

Inez You couldn't care less whether halos are flat or not, you just want to get published.

Hubert Everyone wants to get published, sweetheart, that's the whole point.

Henry If my paper is turned down, I'm finished.

Hubert You are Research Scientist, you have tenure.

Henry An unfireable failure, what could be worse?

Sonia When I married Henry, I imagined – talk about stupid – that there was some ultimate nobility in living among the stars and that it would grant me a certain spiritual loftiness.

Hubert My dear, nothing is in itself elevating or transcendent. Man alone can decide on what he is.

Sonia Brilliant!

Inez Why do you resent my husband?

Sonia I don't resent your husband, it's my husband I resent.

Henry May we know why?

Sonia My husband crawls in front of yours. No normal woman can stand that. Especially when he crawls for no good reason.

Henry I absolutely do not crawl! Do I crawl, Hubert?!

Inez Let's go, Hubert, this is horrifying.

Henry Hubert, do I crawl?!

Sonia You crawl.

Hubert We're all a little tipsy . . .

Sonia Don't try to smooth things over, he crawls in front of you, and you take a malicious pleasure in it, which I can understand . . .

Inez How can you humiliate your husband like this?!

Hubert Inez, stop meddling!

Inez I'll meddle as much as I like, shit!

With brutal abruptness, a song, at maximum volume, starts blaring out of the child's room.

Henry What's that?

Sonia 'The Fox and the Hound.' You put 'The Fox and the Hound' on for him. (*She goes off towards the room.*)

Inez He has his own TV?

Henry Not a TV, a kiddy-cassette player, he's allowed to listen to one kiddy-cassette every evening in bed.

Hubert And if his parents wanted him to watch TV, he'd watch TV!

Inez I didn't say he shouldn't watch TV!

Hubert Yes, you did. You didn't say it but you thought it. You have a propensity for making rules even when it's none of your business.

Inez Did I say he shouldn't watch TV?!

Henry He's not watching TV! He's listening to a little kiddy-cassette in the dark!

Sonia comes back; the music is no longer to be heard.

Sonia He says we're keeping him awake.

Inez He's right, we are keeping him awake, let's go, Hubert.

Henry Before I let you go, Hubert, I want to know if you think I crawl?!

Hubert You're keeping him awake, Henry.

Henry (*lowering his voice*) Do I crawl?

Hubert (*lowering his voice*) A bit.

Henry A bit!

Inez You asked for it! And it's true, you crawl! Hubert, I can't take any more!

Hubert You lack a certain size, Henry, I'm very sorry. You seem somehow adrift, unfocused, maybe you should take a few lessons from your wife. Let's go.

> *They leave.*
> *Henry and Sonia are on their own.*

Two

Evening.
  The same room.
  Sonia is sitting down, wearing a bathrobe. She's looking through a file. Henry appears.
  An atmosphere of calm.

Henry He wants a cookie.

Sonia He just brushed his teeth.

Henry Right.

  Pause.
  She's looking at her file again, he's hovering indecisively.

Henry How about a slice of apple?

Sonia What's the difference between a slice of apple and a cookie?

Henry Less sugar in the apple.

Sonia There's a lot of sugar in an apple. Maybe more than in a cookie.

Henry He often gets hungry in bed, have you noticed? Do you think we feed him too early?

Sonia He eats at six-thirty, like any kid his age.

Henry Suppose he brushed his teeth afterwards?

Sonia What do you mean, 'afterwards'?

Henry After the cookie. He could eat a cookie and brush his teeth afterwards.

Sonia All he has to do is eat a cookie just before going to bed, that is to say, just before brushing his teeth.

Henry Yes.

Sonia You shouldn't have given him that cookie.

Henry I didn't give him anything.

Sonia Yes, you did.

Henry Half a chocolate finger. That's nothing. I was ruthless.

   Slight pause.

So what'll I say to him?

Sonia What'll you say to him?

Henry Should I say no apple?

Sonia You just gave him a chocolate finger. He's not going to get a chocolate finger and an apple.

Henry I'll tell him no apple.

Sonia Tell him no apple, say night-night.

Henry Night-night.

   He goes out and comes back.

He was so sweet. I put on 'The Fox and the Hound' for him. (*Pause.*) What should we give them to start?

Sonia Crudités?

Henry Bit pathetic, isn't it?

Sonia Prosciutto and melon?

Henry With the lamb?

Sonia (*indicating her file*) Listen, Henry . . .

Henry *Prosciutto melone.*

Pause.

What about artichokes?

Sonia Fine.

Henry Artichokes or *prosciutto melone?*

Sonia Henry!

Henry Or what about crab salad? Bit more profile.

Sonia Crab salad. Perfect.

Henry Crab and lamb? . . . Why not? Do you think Finidori's attractive?

Sonia I doubt I've seen him twice in my life.

Henry And did you think he was attractive?

Sonia Arrogant.

Henry Attractive, in other words.

Sonia No, arrogant.

Henry When a woman says arrogant, she means attractive. She might even mean very attractive.

Sonia (*laughing*) Bullshit!

The door buzzer sounds.

(*under her breath*) Who's that?

Henry I'll go look.

He comes back immediately.
All the following exchanges under their breath.

The Finidoris!

Sonia It's tomorrow!

Henry It's the seventeenth . . . it's tonight.

Sonia This is a catastrophe.

Henry Yes.

Sonia What are we going to do?

Henry We can't not let them in.

Sonia I'll go change.

Henry You haven't got time, you're fine like that.

Sonia I'm not going to receive the Finidoris in my bathrobe.

Henry Who gives a fuck? They might as well see you in your bathrobe, all they're gonna get to eat is potato chips.

Sonia I'm not letting them in in my bathrobe!

Henry clings on to her bathrobe as the buzzer sounds again.

Henry You don't have time to change, Sonia!

Sonia (*trying to free herself*) Let me go!

The buzzer sounds again.

Henry How can you be so selfish?

*

Inez, Hubert, Sonia and Henry in the living room.
    The two guests are picking at various snacks (chips, 'Laughing Cow' cheese, a box of chocolate fingers, etc.) set out on a tray. They have drinks, as do Sonia and Henry.
    Sonia has changed. Inez has a run in her pantyhose.

Inez She's alcoholic and depressive. Hubert says it's the same thing but you can be an alcoholic without being a depressive, and depressives aren't all alcoholics, but her, she's both, she takes anti-depressants and she drinks. Anyway she arrived at the house, Bozo the Clown, blotchy foundation, lipstick all over her face, Serge Bloch bringing up the rear, grinning as if everything was all right – except they'd just been flooded out – she'd hardly sat down before she demanded a Scotch, I look at Serge, no reaction!

Brief silence.

Hubert What are you trying to say, darling?

Inez I just want to point out how little you men care about our dignity.

Henry You couldn't live with Serge Bloch and not be a depressive.

Sonia They were flooded out?

Hubert The kid upstairs, before he went on vacation, watered his plants and left the faucet running.

Inez Francine had just redecorated.

Sonia Poor thing! Just her luck!

She laughs heartily. The others join in. Except for Inez.

Hubert Changing the subject, Henry, how far have you gotten with the flatness of halos?

They munch chocolate fingers.

Not bad, these little cookies.

Henry I've finished. I'm submitting the paper before the end of the month.

Hubert Terrific. Having said that, you ought to check on Astro PH, I have the impression a similar piece has been submitted to the *AP-J*.

Henry Recently?

Hubert This morning, a Mexican team. 'On the Flatness of Galaxy Halos.'

Henry 'On the Flatness of Galaxy Halos'!

Sonia (*charmingly*) What's this, Hubert, you're not trying to demoralise my husband?

Hubert In my opinion, Sonia, it would take more than this to demoralise Henry.

Inez So what is your subject?

Henry The same. 'Are the Dark Matter Halos of Galaxies Flat?'

Inez And what does that mean?

Henry There are halos of dark matter in the galaxies, we're trying to establish if they're flattened or spherical.

Inez So which are they?

Hubert Inez, sweetheart, what are these questions, you don't know a thing about it.

Inez I'm interested in Henry's work.

Hubert She's never been interested in mine. You've made a big impression on her, Henry!

Henry I'm doomed.

Sonia (*still cheerful*) Henry, please!

Hubert Let's not exaggerate! I just skimmed over the abstract, maybe they're tackling elliptical galaxies . . .

Henry Have they modelled high-angular momentum systems?

Hubert Possibly.

Henry Then they must be talking about spiral galaxies!

Hubert Maybe they're dealing with visible matter, we don't know what their conclusions might be . . .

Henry I'm doomed! I publish nothing for three years and these bastards beat me to the punch at the very moment I'm about to submit. That's what I call doomed!

The Child Daddy!

Sonia He wants you to rewind the cassette.

Inez How old is he?

Sonia Six.

Inez (*to Henry, who is getting ready to leave the room*) May I see him?

Henry Come with me.

> *They go out.*
> *Hubert and Sonia are on their own.*

Hubert That gives me exactly fifteen seconds to persuade you to have lunch with me this week.

Sonia That's more than enough.

Hubert Tomorrow?

Sonia I can't, tomorrow.

Hubert Monday?

Sonia All right.

Hubert Are you coming for his sake or mine?

Sonia For his sake, of course.

Hubert Perfect!

Sonia Why tell him about that paper?

Hubert Sudden inspiration. To spice up the evening.

Sonia So you made it up?

Hubert No.

Sonia Is it serious?

Hubert Depends.

He seizes her hand and lifts it boldly to his lips.

Sonia On what?

Hubert His approach.

Sonia I'll tell him everything.

Hubert Goodbye Grade A!

Sonia laughs.

Sonia He asked me if I found you attractive.

Hubert Did you say 'very'?

Sonia I said 'arrogant'.

Hubert Good, much more subtle.

Sonia In your circle, do you pass for attractive?

Hubert There's very little competition.

Sonia You have no shame?

Hubert Shame?

Sonia In my home. Three feet away from your wife.

Hubert My morality is not dictated by distance.

Sonia What is it dictated by?

Hubert You'll find out on Monday.

Inez (*on her way back*) He said, 'I don't want her in my room.' I said, 'Hello, Arnaud,' he turned to his father and said, 'I don't want her in my room.' Don't worry about it, I have two of my own, not to mention nephews, I'm not in the least upset.

Sonia I hope Henry gave him a hard time.

Inez I need a drink. Thank God, Henry did not give him a hard time, he's peeling him an apple.

Sonia I break my neck to get him to brush his teeth and the next minute Henry's stuffing him with food.

Inez All men do that.

Hubert What's this stupid generalisation about men? Where do you get these ideas, Inez? Personally, I've never stuffed anyone with food.

Inez You get them all worked up, which is worse. He can start a game of soccer when they're just about to get into bed.

Hubert Once, I played soccer with them. She's going to be talking about it for the next ten years.

Sonia You play soccer? It's funny, I never imagined you playing soccer.

Hubert I don't play soccer, I kick the ball around from time to time with my sons, Inez calls that playing soccer. How did you imagine me?

Sonia I didn't imagine you. Your husband's a little full of himself, isn't he?

Inez My husband likes to provoke. If there's a pretty woman in the room, he'll give us his lady-killer.

Hubert The Sancerre going down well, darling?

Henry (*coming back*) I found some Cheez-Its, I'm so embarrassed, there's a can of sardines as well, would you like me to open the sardines?

Hubert Cheez-Its, fantastic. Perhaps I should have gone easier on the chocolate fingers.

Sonia You gave him an apple?

Henry I peeled him a small apple. He's hungry, if he's hungry in bed, what else am I supposed to do?

Sonia You'd already given him a chocolate finger.

Henry Half a chocolate finger. Let's not start this conversation again, Sonia, it can't be very interesting for our guests.

Hubert Don't you believe it, Henry, a brush with a couple's private life, pretty stimulating.

Henry Perhaps, if you were to find a less mundane example.

Hubert That's exactly what's exciting about it. Mundane private life. You can't always fix your mind on higher planes.

Inez Personally, I'm more mentally engaged in a discussion on the advisability of half a chocolate finger than on the flatness of galaxies.

Hubert Halos, darling.

Henry If we could possibly avoid this subject, if we could possibly completely banish this subject for the evening, I'd be extremely grateful.

Hubert You're tormenting yourself for no good reason, Henry.

YASMINA REZA

Henry I'm not tormenting myself in the slightest, you've been kind enough to inform me of the existence of a parallel study, I've taken note of it, the subject is closed.

Sonia Hubert, it's your job to reassure my husband. You're responsible for his disarray.

Henry Please, Sonia, will you stop making me out to be someone who gets demoralised at the drop of a hat and who has no backbone whatsoever. Everything's fine, we've just got rid of two unpromising subjects, and somewhere between apples and dark matter, I'm sure we can find some new, more beguiling topic.

Hubert Last month, I left to spend a few days at an international conference in Finland. I rubbed shoulders with the best teams in the world. I attended some extraordinary seminars, I gave one myself which was fortunately considered significant, I had the most fruitful encounters with various great pundits, and what do I remember? What was it that impressed itself on my mind and, at the risk of seeming pompous, my soul? A drab and lugubrious walk on the outskirts of Turku. I rubbed shoulders with the greatest American, English and Dutch researchers, we had these remarkable encounters, and what remains? A dreary walk beside a grey sea.

Pause.

Inez May we know why you're suddenly telling us this?

Hubert It's an echo of what Henry was saying. I was thinking about the relative importance of things. About what's interesting and what isn't. Seemingly empty moments stay incised in the memory, trivial words can engage your whole being. Henry? . . .

Sonia Henry? . . . Hubert is making an effort to find us a beguiling subject.

Henry Very beguiling, yes. Go on.

Hubert I've finished.

Slight pause.

Inez Have you lived here long?

Sonia A year and a half.

Inez Where were you before?

Sonia Montparnasse.

Inez This is better. Quieter.

Henry It's certainly not quiet, they're building a parking lot in Rue Langelot.

Inez It'll be finished at some point.

Henry In two years.

Sonia (*laughing*) Next month!

Inez Do you mind if I smoke?

Henry I'd rather you didn't.

Sonia What's bugging you, you're kidding! Of course you can smoke, Inez!

Hubert No one's smoking, why do you have to smoke?

Sonia She can absolutely smoke, Henry, tell her she can smoke!

Hubert We're in Henry's apartment, cigarettes make Henry uncomfortable, there's no reason Inez should smoke. In fact, smoking is never essential for a woman.

Inez I won't smoke.

Sonia Inez, I insist that you smoke.

Inez I don't feel like smoking any more.

Sonia Are you planning to be bad-tempered and rude all evening, Henry?

Henry Smoke, fuck it.

Hubert Henry, I don't want to rub salt in the wound, but you have to admit something's gone wrong with this evening.

A muffled song is heard, coming from the child's room.

Inez You have 'The Fox and the Hound'!

Henry Your walk in Finland really fucking depressed me.

Inez Our children have that too.

Henry In my position, Hubert, ludicrous as it may seem, an invitation to Turku is an end in itself. And someone who sees the conference as an end in itself has trouble getting his head around some existential stroll along the Baltic. Should he be listening to a tape this late?

Sonia You just rewound it for him.

Inez Doesn't he know how to rewind his own cassettes?

Sonia He's too lazy to move.

Inez Really?

Hubert 'Luminous and Dark Matter in Spiral Galaxies', that was the subject of the conference. Why didn't you sign up for it?

Henry To stand there in front of a wall poster? And spend twenty-four hours on the sidelines, like Serge Bloch in Edinburgh?

Hubert Your work on the dynamics of galaxies is well known, you'd have had no difficulty getting yourself invited, Henry. Dynamicists were welcome in Turku.

Henry Stop being so condescending. If you don't mind.
Stop trying to throw me a lifeline every two minutes.
I don't give a fuck about Turku.

Hubert You've just said the opposite.

Henry I don't give a fuck about Turku.

Sonia Stop it, Henry, this is childish. And embarrassing.

Henry I don't give a fuck about Turku.

Sonia Right, he doesn't give a fuck about Turku, and
I wouldn't mind another splash of wine.

Hubert You do give a fuck about Turku, and about your
paper, and about your promotion, but you think it's
clever – God knows why – to self-destruct out of pride.

Henry You're right, I'm self-destructing in front of you
and I'm enjoying it. An hour ago I was all set to kiss
your feet, now I'm experiencing the elation of the
convert.

Sonia You've had too much to drink, Henry. You're
blind drunk.

Henry What? I thought you'd be delighted, darling.
Farewell the Finidorian tone. Farewell the head hung
low and the hunched shoulders, farewell the servile
chuckle . . .

Inez What is the Finidorian tone?

Henry A tone of voice I used to adopt when I believed
Hubert Finidori was in a position to determine my
future, before he arrived at my apartment a day early
and lost no time – no time whatsoever! – in giving me
a piece of disturbing information, in the vaguest and
therefore most disturbing way, and, seeing how disturbed
I was, backtracked marginally in order to restore me to

reason and then, just to finish the job and steamroller me completely, started boasting about the futility, emptiness and pointlessness of success.

Inez If we did come a day early, Henry, it's entirely my fault. I wrote down Thursday the seventeenth on a scrap of paper when the seventeenth is a Friday – usually on Fridays I have my class at . . .

Hubert We don't give a shit, Inez, we don't give a shit, it's not important. You're a real artist, Henry, you make and unmake the world according to your mood. You raised me to the rank of protector, I had no idea. I had no idea you'd inflicted this status on me. Had I known, I'd have made an effort to inform you of my power-lessness. You see, I didn't notice the servile chuckle, and, fool that I am, I discerned a hint of friendship in what was actually the Finidorian tone. I'm sorry you feel so bitter and I'm sorry I can't take responsibility for it, because I had no idea who I was in your eyes.

Inez You had a very clear idea, Hubert, and I've had enough of being insulted every time I open my mouth. Just now, in the street, my husband told me Henry needed his support if he wanted to be made Research Director.

Hubert I did not say, my darling, that Henry needed my support, I said, but you were concentrating on the run in your pantyhose (which by the way is getting worse), I said, in a spirit of solidarity, that I could conceivably, if Henry managed to publish within the year, give a modest nudge to his promotion prospects. I said it without suspecting this task had already been assigned to me and I said it in the way a man does when he's speaking to his wife in the privacy of a close and trusting relationship.

Sonia Your nerve is disarming. Is this all part of your seductiveness?

Henry Your seductiveness, Hubert! What about that?

Inez You said Henry needed your support. And you also said he and his wife would be licking our boots.

Hubert I was wrong! As you can see, they're by no means licking our boots.

Henry I'm not licking your boots, because I delight in disappointing people, and as for my wife, I doubt she'd ever lick anyone's boots for my benefit. There are no more chocolate fingers, have you scarfed the entire box?

Sonia Don't have any more to drink, Henry.

Henry I really like your tie, Hubert, it's something I noticed right away, the splendour of your tie and its failure to match your pocket handkerchief, a remarkably bold gesture, not to mention the very fact of the tie itself, rare in our field, where slovenliness is just one informality among many, but you, Hubert, you're a man from another mould, a man with bearing, remote, formal, melancholy on a northern coastline . . . To be such an insignificant part of the universe and yet to feel the urge to sound your note, your infinitesimal note in the bell-tower of eternity.

Inez Well, as far as I'm concerned – I've drunk as much as you have, Henry, so here goes – I don't agree at all. You'll probably laugh, but what's the difference, my husband snickers or sighs every time I open my mouth – our relationship's going down the toilet, we may as well admit it – I don't agree at all that man is insignificant in the universe. What would the universe be without us? A gloomy place, a black place, without an ounce of poetry. It's us who named it, it's us, Man, who gave this labyrinth black holes, dead light, infinity, eternity, things that no one can see, it's us who've made it so dazzling. We're not nothing, our time may be short, but we're not nothing . . .

Brief silence.

Sonia You said we'd be licking your boots? I'm sorry to bring things down to earth when Inez has made a valiant attempt to raise the level of debate.

Hubert Licking our boots? Is that a turn of phrase from my vocabulary book?

Inez You said licking our boots.

Hubert I said *licking our boots*, Inez? What does licking our boots mean? Servile, or quite simply, courteous, well brought up? For some obscure reason, Inez stabs me in the back, she flings up some out-of-context remark in the driest and most withering way and I'm supposed to come up with some response? Surely, dear friends, we're not about to lapse into the completely abject?

Sonia Give up this flatulent tone, Hubert, you're the only one who finds it amusing. You said we'd be licking your boots, and in the phrase, let me point out, it's the 'we' which is particularly unfortunate. I can understand you might envision the supplicant licking your boots, that might even be what constitutes the charm of a supplicant, but to include his wife in this tableau of prostration is a mistake. I did find you somewhat intriguing, I must admit, I wasn't expecting you to be so crass and ordinary.

Henry And you can drop that tone as well, Sonia! What's all this simpering? The charm of a supplicant? If you go on like that, the supplicant might very well punch your face in!

Hubert You're out of control, Henry!

Inez He's not out of control.

Sonia What's the matter with you, Inez?

Inez I saw you just now.

Sonia Saw who?

Inez The two of you.

Sonia Saw what?

Inez You know very well.

Hubert Inez, come down to earth, sweetheart. Inez can't drink more than one glass, after that she can no longer navigate the known universe.

Sonia Saw what? Say it.

Inez You're too strong for me, Sonia, I'm so easily demolished . . .

> *She holds out her glass to Henry, who fills it and empties his own glass.*

Inez Thank you, Henry.

Hubert I'll take her home.

Inez It's going to be hideous in the car – you see, Henry, here he holds back, he behaves like a gentleman, but in the car it'll be a nightmare. Would you mind calling me a taxi?

Henry Saw what, Sonia? What did she see?

Sonia What did she see? I don't know! She won't tell us!

Hubert She saw nothing, she's had a little too much to drink and she's going to go home and go quietly to bed . . .

Inez (*to Henry*) They're just like each other, they have the same cynicism and the same self-assurance. We can't compete with people like that.

Henry Don't put us in the same category! Don't even think of trying to lump us together! You and I come from separate worlds!

Inez That's what you think . . .

Hubert Let's go.

Henry Fuck off. Take your Hausfrau. And fuck off.

Inez Wonderful, Henry! Call me all the names you can think of, I've gone through the drunkenness barrier, I look like a gypsy, my husband's a swine, for me this is a historic evening

Hubert Let's go.

Inez Yes, let's go, sweetheart, you can finish me off in the Audi, we have a new Audi, Hubert parked very carefully about a mile away so it wouldn't get scratched . . .

Hubert You're like Francine Bloch, Inez, you're not going to give us your Francine Bloch, are you, darling?

Inez I'm unhumiliatable, say what you like . . .

Henry And no snivelling! For God's sake! Don't go sentimentalising everything with all this bourgeois whining. Unhumiliatable! I like the word, don't get me wrong, its my kind of word, great position to be in, unhumiliatable, fuck off.

Hubert Let's go. (*He drags Inez away.*) See you soon, Sonia.

Sonia Goodbye.

Hubert Monday?

Sonia Absolutely not.

He smiles at her.
Hubert and Inez leave.
Henry and Sonia are on their own.

Three

Evening. The four of them (the Finidoris have arrived).
The same situation. Sonia is in her bathrobe.
Inez has no run in her pantyhose. The atmosphere
seems enjoyable.

Hubert When we talk about String Theory, the Theory
of Everything, what do we mean? We mean a unifying
theory of all the fundamental forces. However, even if
you could conceive a theory which covered all the basic
interactions, for one thing your theory would be far
from comprehensive. As Poincaré said, you can examine
each individual cell of an elephant, but that won't help
you grasp its zoological reality, and you still wouldn't
have eliminated the paradox of the cosmos! How can we
grasp the world as it is? How can we close the gap
between reality and representation, the gap between
object and word, what are these, fingers, delicious – how,
in short, can we think of the world without our thinking
being part of the world?

Henry All the more tragic a paradox since the principal
aim of scientific enterprise is total objectivity.

Hubert Following religion and philosophy, science is now
chasing the idea of unity. Is it a hopeless pursuit or the
Promised Land?

Henry Who can say?

Sonia What's the aim of a unifying theory?

Hubert It's a good question. A very good question, but
I don't know if it's right to speak of aims rather than

longings. Our life is full of regrets for an integrated world, nostalgia for some lost wholeness, nostalgia which is accentuated by the fragmentation of the world brought about by modern life.

Henry Precisely.

A muffled song is heard, coming from the child's room.

Inez 'The Fox and the Hound'!

Henry How come he's still awake?

Sonia He's awake. You can't force him to sleep. He turned off the light and he's listening to his cassette.

Inez He's sweet. Very independent.

Sonia Yes, he's very independent.

Inez You're lucky, ours are capable of showing up fourteen times in the course of the evening.

Henry Arnaud is completely self-sufficient. Too much so, possibly. If you ask me, it's time he turned off his cassette, don't you think, Sonitchka?

Sonia (*getting up, to Inez*) Would you like to see him?

Inez Love to!

They go out.
Hubert and Henry are on their own.

Hubert So, the flatness of halos?

Henry Finished. I'm submitting the paper end of the month.

Hubert Great. Having said that, you ought to check on Astro PH, I have the impression a similar piece has been accepted by the *AP-J*.

Henry That's right, 'On the Flatness of Dark Halos in Galaxies'. Raoul Arestegui, a colleague of mine, called to tell me about it, I left my laptop at the Institute.

Hubert Pretty close to your subject, isn't it? These cookies are a disaster, take them away.

Henry No, please, eat, I'm embarrassed to serve you this way. It's precisely my subject, apparently it's *the* fashionable subject, a Mexican team.

Hubert So the Mexicans are at it!

Henry That's right!

Hubert Is that a problem?

Henry I hope not. I don't know what their approach is or their conclusion. Raoul's going to call me back. There's a good chance we may complement each other.

Hubert Yes, yes, yes. I'm sure you will.

Henry Let's put our trust in the diversity of the human brain.

Hubert Good for you.

Henry I'll have to incorporate their results in my paper. Might even be an advantage.

Hubert Sure! I've got to say, Henry, you're in very good shape.

Henry Exhausted, but, yes, in good shape.

Hubert Nice part of town.

Henry Very.

Sonia appears.

Sonia He wants you to come.

Henry I'd rather he went to sleep.

Sonia He's showing Inez his airport and he says you haven't seen it.

Henry Would you excuse me for two minutes, Hubert?

> *He goes out.*
> *Hubert and Sonia are on their own.*
> *Immediately, Hubert throws himself at Sonia and tries to take her in his arms.*

Hubert Half-undressed, no make-up, in your apartment, surrounded by your things, you couldn't have done better if you'd planned to knock me off my feet . . .

Sonia (*laughing and trying – feebly – to get away from him*) You're crazy . . .

Hubert (*pursuing her*) You're adorable, Sonia, you're heart-breaking, you're disarming. . . I didn't run here, I flew here, I blasted a day out of the calendar, I dismantled time to get back by your side . . .

Sonia You've seen me twice in your life . . . you're drunk . . .

Hubert So? Once would have been enough . . .

> *He tries to kiss her, misses. She laughs, pulls away. He catches hold of her hand, playful.*

Do you know the Baltic? . . . Last month I went for a walk north of Turku, through cold and desolate countryside, and all I could think of was a woman glimpsed when I was visiting Serge Bloch and his unfortunate wife.

> *She manages to escape, but he recaptures her.*

I was walking beside a dark sea, beside low houses with no windows, and I couldn't stop thinking of her . . .

what a lucky man Henry is, Henry is magnificent, some Mexicans have covered his subject, he couldn't care less, if they refuse to publish his paper, there's nothing I can do for him . . . I worship your eyes . . .

Sonia Mexicans?

Hubert Mexicans.

Sonia They're the other side of that door . . .

Hubert The Mexicans?

Sonia laughs and lets herself be caught.

Sonia . . . My son, Henry, Inez.

Hubert The whole world is on the other side of that door . . . the world is always on the other side of the door!

He kisses her. She lets him do it.
The voices of lnez and Henry can be heard.
They pull apart.

Inez He's a real architect, that child!

Henry He wants a cookie.

Hubert (*grabbing the box of chocolate fingers*) Here, take these fingers, they'll be the death of me!

Inez Really, Hubert, they're not going to give him a box of cookies in bed!

Henry Not even one!

Sonia Give it to him, what harm can it do, it's not going to kill him.

Henry Give him the whole box?

Hubert I've eaten three-quarters of them.

Inez (*to Henry, who's about to leave the room with the box*) You're wrong, Henry.

Henry What should I do?

Sonia Give him a cookie.

Henry Just one?

Hubert There can't be more than two or three left in the box.

Henry What should I do, Sonia, before I go crazy?

Sonia Give him what's left and tell him it'll never happen again.

   Henry goes out.

Inez He explained it all to me. In fact, he's built an airport station . . .

Hubert An airport terminal.

Inez No, no, an airport station.

Hubert The word is 'terminal'.

Inez I know perfectly well what a terminal is, Hubert, but the child has built an airport station, a station inside an airport, a station with trains, with tracks crossing the runways, it's not a terminal, it's an airport with airplanes, combined with a railroad station and he calls it an airport station . . .!

Henry (*coming back*) There were two fingers left!

Inez What is that thing Arnaud has made? An airport station!

Henry That's right, an airport station!

Hubert All right. You don't have to get annoyed.

Henry Who's getting annoyed? You must be dying of thirst out here. Something stronger, Hubert?

Hubert No, thanks, I'll stick with the Sancerre.

Henry *(serving him)* Sonia? . . . Inez? . . .

Refills everyone's glass. Inez drinks.
Silence.

Hubert What's happening with the Blochs? Have you seen them?

Sonia They've been flooded out.

Hubert Flooded out?

Sonia The kid upstairs, before he went on vacation, watered his plants and left the faucet running.

Henry Francine had just redecorated.

Sonia And he'd just come out of a depression.

Hubert Poor man's a depressive.

Henry Yes.

Pause.

Hubert The last time I saw him, I said, listen, Serge, depression is a spiral, no one can help you, no one can do a thing for you, the only cure is willpower, willpower, willpower. After that, he was three times worse. Not at all the right thing to say to him. He was prostrate when I left, I've never seen anyone look so terrified.

Inez If I was depressed and somebody said to me willpower, willpower, I'd jump right out a window.

Sonia Me too.

Hubert What can you say? You're behind the eight-ball whatever you do. You could say you're ahead of the game, Serge, you've pre-empted the inevitable decay, good job, be grateful to your destiny for giving you the edge in this kingdom of the damned. You could say that.

Silence.

Henry We ought to ask the Blochs for dinner.

Sonia Any other brilliant ideas?

The telephone rings.
Henry answers it.

Henry Hello, yes . . . (to *the others*) It's Raoul Arestegui . . . (*to Raoul*) Yes . . . yes . . . Right. Really? . . . Really! . . . No, no, I dealt with three of the external galaxies! . . . You said it! . . . One to ten . . . Three to four? . . . Good, wonderful . . . Thanks, Raoul, thank you, I can't talk now, I'm with some friends, see you Monday . . . Ciao. (*He hangs up.*) 'On the Flatness of the Milky Way's Dark Halo.' The Milky Way! They've dealt with the Milky Way! . . . Cosmological simulations give a ratio of one to two! My ratio is one to ten! And the Mexicans' results are three to four!

Hubert Fantastic.

Henry (*quietly crazed with joy*) Not so fantastic, but I do feel better! Come on, everyone, drink up! Here's to the Mexicans! You must be starving to death? Sonia, where are those Cheez-Its, didn't we have some Cheez-Its, darling?

Sonia There . . .

Henry Ah, I hadn't spotted them! Cheddar Jack Cheez-Its, Hot and Spicy Cheez-Its! Hot and Spicy, fabulous, Inez?

Inez No, thank you.

Henry Come on, Hubert, eat!

Hubert takes a handful of Cheez-Its and raises his glass.

Hubert To the publication of your paper, Henry!

Henry (*clinking his glass, happy*) He's busting my chops, but I don't mind!

Inez I don't know what you're talking about, but here's to you, anyway!

Sonia Here's to you and here's a kiss, my love.

Henry Yes, kiss me, my love! And we'll raise our glasses to the hero of the hour, that colossus who's published nothing for three years and who's painting the town red because he's able to submit his little paper!

Sonia Don't be so coy!

Henry Not coy. Flippant, Sonia. I don't want our friends to think that, in spite of my relief, I've lost all sense of proportion. (*He drinks.*) Especially in front of a pundit.

Hubert He's busting my chops, but what do I care?

Sonia You're not a pundit? I'd be very disappointed.

Henry Be careful, I've steeped her in the myth of Finidori.

Hubert I see.

Henry The Milky Way! Idiot, why didn't he tell me right away? Here I was, worrying about spiral galaxies and elliptical galaxies! Some music? Let's put on some music!

Inez Oh, yes, some music!

Sonia Henry . . . we're not putting on any music, Henry!

Henry Why not?

Hubert He's right, why not?

Henry No, of course, this is stupid, we shouldn't put on any music.

Inez Why shouldn't we put on some music?

Hubert He doesn't want to any more, Inez.

Sonia We can spend an enjoyable evening without music, can't we?

Inez You seem depressed all of a sudden, Henry.

Henry I'm not depressed.

Inez Your son built a wonderful thing, tomorrow, he'll destroy it, in his world you don't keep things, you keep nothing, not even yourself . . . (*She drinks.*) Give me another glass, Henry, please, I'm feeling low suddenly, I'm afraid I might even spoil your evening . . . He made snow on the runways with tissues . . . above the building blocks he made storms, and hurricanes . . . above us . . . what is there? . . . You live up in the stars, Henry. Tell me there's not nothing.

Henry I don't live up in the stars, Inez . . . Far lower down, if you want to know the truth.

Inez Really?

Henry As you can see. Sliding from an absurd euphoria to an equally absurd melancholy. It's all built on nothing.

Slight pause.

Hubert Anyway, Henry, getting back to your paper, providing you publish before the end of the year, I'll make a point of mentioning you to the Committee.

Henry No obligation whatsoever, Hubert.

Sonia Henry, are you sure you haven't had a little too much to drink?

Hubert I'll mention you, because you're very pure, you're talented but not in the least aggressive. You don't have the strategic capabilities of a number of your colleagues. A career is a plan of campaign.

Henry Put that way, it makes me want to puke.

Hubert In that case, I'll mention you in order to get into Sonia's good graces, since I get the impression she doesn't like me.

Inez You think you're witty but you're so obvious.

Sonia The elegant way to go about it would have been to support my husband without letting him know. A discreet leg-up.

Hubert So you don't like me.

Henry Who wants the last Hot and Spicy Cheez-It?

Hubert You eat it, Henry.

Pause.

Henry The Hot and Spicy ones are my favourites.

Hubert For me, the discovery of the evening was . . . what are they called? . . . fingers. Make a note of them, Inez.

Henry You'll be able to brag about going to the shittiest dinner party of your life.

Hubert This sudden bout of gloom, Henry, give me a hint. Is it something to do with us?

Sonia Henry wants things to happen and he wants them not to happen. He wants to succeed and at the same time not to succeed, to be somebody and to be nobody. To be you, Hubert, and to be a failure. He wants to be helped and he wants to be rejected. That's Henry for you, Hubert, a man who slides from euphoria to melancholy and from melancholy back to euphoria, who suddenly gets excited, leaps out of bed and gets excited and thinks life is full of promise and sees himself getting the Russell Medal or the Nobel, takes on a feverishly conspiratorial air, then, suddenly, for no reason, is overwhelmed and paralysed, so that haste and impatience are replaced by doubt and insecurity and desire is replaced by doubt and boundless insecurity. Some people can cope with life and some people can't . . .

Inez I have a run in my hose.

Henry She used to be a lawyer before she went to work for the finance company. If you ask me, any criminal you can think of, she would have gotten him off.

Hubert Why don't you put your glass down, Inez?

Inez I've wilted in two hours. Did you know Hubert's just been elected to the Academy of Science?

Silence.

Sonia You've just been elected to the Academy of Science?

Hubert You don't have to shout it from the rooftops.

Inez This isn't the rooftops, we're with our friends.

Hubert Our friends couldn't care less.

Sonia Your friends could care less, Hubert, your friends – if the word is not an exaggeration – your friends are very impressed. They bow down. They would like to share your delight but . . .

Henry They do share your delight, well done, Hubert, what's she talking about?!

Sonia They do share your delight, yes.

Henry We share your delight. The Academy, what an achievement, Hubert! And here we are celebrating the Academy with chips and Cheez-Its! We do share your delight, and even if this evening I'm suddenly prone, you know, to some slight feeling of isolation, I'm delighted, Hubert, sincerely I am, at your apotheosis.

Hubert Apotheosis. Right. (*He gets up.*) Inez. It's late, we have to be going.

    Inez gets up.

Hubert I will speak to the Committee about you, Henry. Discreetly. Send me your paper even before you submit it.

Inez Thanks for a lovely evening. It's time I went, only takes one glass to make me feel tipsy.

Hubert Goodbye, Sonia . . .

Sonia Goodbye . . .

    They leave.
    Henry and Sonia are on their own.
    Silence.

Henry Is he asleep?

Sonia Think so.

    'The Fox and the Hound' music is heard, coming from the child's room.